Springer Texts in Business and Economics

For further volumes:
http://www.springer.com/series/10099

Ulrich Schreiber

International Company Taxation

An Introduction to the Legal and Economic Principles

In cooperation with Peter Müller

Springer

Ulrich Schreiber
Business School
University of Mannheim
Mannheim, Germany

ISSN 2192-4333 ISSN 2192-4341 (electronic)
ISBN 978-3-642-36305-4 ISBN 978-3-642-36306-1 (eBook)
DOI 10.1007/978-3-642-36306-1
Springer Heidelberg New York Dordrecht London

Library of Congress Control Number: 2013931189

Printed on acid-free paper

Springer is part of Springer Science+Business Media (www.springer.com)

Preface

This book offers an introduction to the legal and economic fundamentals of international company taxation. It is written for students of business economics and tax law striving to understand how taxes influence investment and financing decisions in cross-border situations. The focus of the book is on the key tax drivers shaping the tax planning strategies of multinational companies. Special attention is given to the specifics of the European internal market.

I would like to thank the research assistants who have read earlier versions of the book and, in particular, Dieter Endres and Andrew Miles for their great support.

Mannheim, November 2012 Ulrich Schreiber

Contents

List of Symbols XI

Abbreviations XV

List of Tables XVII

1. International Company Taxation 1
   1.1. Legal Structures of Company Taxation 1
      1.1.1. Legally Distinct Entities 1
      1.1.2. Pass-Through Entities 3
   1.2. Corporation Tax 4
      1.2.1. Corporation Tax Base 4
      1.2.2. Corporation Tax Rates 6
      1.2.3. Corporation Tax System 8
      1.2.4. Group Taxation 10
   1.3. International Double Taxation 11
      1.3.1. Limited and Unlimited Tax Liability 11
      1.3.2. Legal Double Taxation 12
      1.3.3. OECD Model Treaty 14
   1.4. International Profit Allocation 17
      1.4.1. Transfer Pricing 17
         1.4.1.1. Market Prices 17
         1.4.1.2. Subsidiary 18
         1.4.1.3. Permanent Establishment 20
      1.4.2. Cross-border Reorganization 22

2. Fundamentals of International Tax Planning 27
   2.1. Cash Flow and Net Present Value 27
      2.1.1. Equity Financed Investments 27
      2.1.2. Debt Financed Investments 32
   2.2. Investment Shifting and Profit Shifting 35
   2.3. International Tax Planning and Residence-Based Taxation 37
   2.4. International Tax Planning and Source-Based Taxation 40
   2.5. International Tax Planning under Hybrid Tax Systems 42
   2.6. Legal Restrictions on Tax Planning 46
      2.6.1. General Anti-Abuse Rules 46
      2.6.2. Specific Anti-Abuse Rules 48
         2.6.2.1. Controlled Foreign Corporations Legislation 48
         2.6.2.2. Thin Capitalization Rules 48

3. International Corporate Tax Planning....... 51
3.1. Tasks of International Corporate Tax Planning....... 51
3.2. Investment Decisions....... 52
3.2.1. Legal Form....... 52
3.2.2. Investment Location....... 55
3.2.3. Acquisitions....... 58
3.2.4. Allocation of Ownership Rights....... 63
3.2.5. Loss Compensation....... 67
3.2.6. Transfer Pricing....... 70
3.2.6.1. Subsidiary....... 70
3.2.6.2. Permanent Establishment....... 73
3.2.7. Outbound Transfer of Assets....... 76
3.3. Financing Decisions....... 79
3.3.1. Internal Debt....... 79
3.3.2. External Debt....... 83
3.3.3. Profit Repatriation....... 86
3.4. Special Purpose Entities....... 90
3.4.1. Finance Companies....... 90
3.4.2. Holding Companies....... 92
3.5. Empirical Evidence on International Tax Planning....... 94

4. International Taxation and European Law....... 99
4.1. Fundamental Freedoms and Income Taxation....... 99
4.2. Freedom of Establishment....... 100
4.2.1. Scope....... 100
4.2.2. Prohibited Restriction....... 101
4.2.3. Justifications....... 102
4.2.4. Proportionality....... 103
4.3. EU Law and International Tax Planning....... 104
4.3.1. Cross-Border Loss Compensation....... 104
4.3.1.1. Foreign Subsidiaries....... 104
4.3.1.2. Foreign Permanent Establishments....... 105
4.3.2. Dividend Taxation....... 106
4.3.3. Debt Financing....... 108
4.3.3.1. Internal Debt Financing....... 108
4.3.3.2. External Debt Financing....... 109
4.3.4. Income Tax Deferral....... 111
4.3.5. Outbound Transfer of Assets....... 112

5. Corporate Tax Harmonization in the European Union....... 117
5.1. Common Consolidated Corporate Tax Base....... 117
5.2. Profit Allocation....... 119
5.2.1. Scope of the Group and Determination of Profits....... 119
5.2.2. Formula Apportionment....... 121

5.3. Entering and Leaving the Group 127
5.3.1. Transfer of Assets 127
5.3.2. Transfer of Shares 129
5.3.3. Business Reorganizations 130
5.4. Non-EU Countries 131

6. International Tax Planning and Accounting for Income Taxes 135
6.1. The Role of Income Tax Reporting 135
6.2. The Effective Tax Rate 136
6.2.1. Cash Flow Based Effective Tax Rate 136
6.2.2. Accounting Based Effective Tax Rate 140
6.3. Determination of Deferred Taxes 142
6.4. Tax Reconciliation Statement 145
6.5. Effective Tax Rate and International Tax Planning 147

Literature 151

Index 159

List of Symbols

α_F	Factor of tax recognition in the foreign country
α_H	Factor of tax recognition in the home country
α_{MS}^C	Factor of weight for capital in Member State MS
α_{MS}^L	Factor of weight for wages in Member State MS
α_{MS}^S	Factor of weight for sales in Member State MS
β_1	Factor of weight for payroll
β_2	Factor of weight for employees
BV_0	Book value of an asset at $t = 0$
C	Overall group capital
C_0	Net present value before taxes
C_0^τ	Net present value after taxes
$C_0^{\tau,F}$	Net present value of a foreign depreciable asset after taxes
$C_0^{\tau,H}$	Net present value of a domestic depreciable asset after taxes
$C_0^{\tau,IP}$	Net present value of IP company after taxes
$C_0^{\tau,R\&D}$	Net present value of R&D company after taxes
C_{MS}	Capital in Member State MS
CF_t	Cash flow at time t
CF_z	Cash flow at time $z = t+1$
ΔCF_n	Difference in cash flow at time $t = n$
D_t	Depreciation at time t
DIV_t	Dividend payment at time t
DIV_T	Pre-tax dividend of Company T
DIV_B^τ	After-tax dividend received by B Corporation´s shareholders
DIV_S^τ	After-tax dividend received by S Corporation´s shareholders
ED_t	Economic depreciation at time t
EP_t	Economic profit at time t
F_{MS}	Total share of profit of Member State MS
HR_0	Hidden reserves of an asset at time $t = 0$
I	Interest paid
I_0	Initial investment outlay
i	Market interest rate
i_τ	Market interest rate after taxes
$i_{\tau,CF}$	After-tax rate of return of a foreign corporation
L	Overall group wages
L_{MS}	Wages in Member State MS

L_t	Debt at time t
LCF_t	Loss carry-forward at time t
LS_t	Losses deducted from the tax base at time t
MV_0	Market value of an asset in $t = 0$
m	Profit mark-up
N	Overall number of employees
N_{MS}	Number of employees in Member State MS
$NPVP_0$	Net present value of economic profits at time $t = 0$
$NPVT_0$	Net present value of taxes at $t = 0$
n_H	Periods of deferred exit taxation
π	Overall group profit
P_B	Maximum price of Corporation B
P_S	Minimum price of Corporation S
PR	Perpetual profit
PR_T	Pre-tax cash flow of Company T
PV_0	Present value of cash flow before taxes at $t = 0$
PV_0^τ	Present value of cash flow after taxes at $t = 0$
PV_t	Net present value of pre-tax cash-flows at time t
PVL_0^τ	Net present value of debt capital after taxes at time $t = 0$
p	Pre-tax rate of return
$q(i, \tau_{I,B}, n)$	After-tax discount factor for $t = n$
$R\ (i, \tau_{I,S}, n)$	Annuity factor for $t = n$
r	Rate of return
r_D	Pre-tax rate of return of a domestic investment
r_F	Pre-tax rate of return of a foreign investment
S	Overall group sales
S_{MS}	Sales in Member State MS
T_t	Tax liability at time t
TC_t	Corporation tax liability at time t
TD_t	Shareholder tax liability on dividends at time t
TET_0	Total tax effect of an asset transfer at time $t = 0$
TP_t	Taxable profit at time t
T_{MS}	Tax liability in Member State MS
TS	Tax shield
τ	Individual income tax rate
τ_B	Income tax rate of the buyer
τ_C	Combined corporation tax rate
τ_{CF}	Corporation tax rate foreign subsidiary
$\tau_{CG,B}$	Individual capital gains tax rate in Country B
τ_{CH}	Corporation tax rate domestic subsidiary
τ_D	Individual dividend tax rate
$\tau_{D,B}$	Individual income tax rate on dividends in Country B
$\tau_{D,S}$	Individual income tax rate on dividends in Country S
τ_F	Foreign income tax rate

τ_{FI}	Tax rate for financial investments
τ_G	Average group tax rate
τ_H	Domestic income tax rate
τ_I	Tax rate for interest income
$\tau_{I,B}$	Individual income tax rate on interest income in Country B
$\tau_{I,S}$	Individual income tax rate on interest income in Country S
τ_L	Income tax rate in Country L
τ_{MS}	Statutory tax rate in Member State MS
τ_P	Tax rate on business profits
τ_{RI}	Statutory tax rate for real investments
τ_S	Income tax rate of the seller
τ_T	Profit tax rate of Company T
t	Time
V	Pre-tax value of a target company
V^τ	After-tax value of a target company
V_B^τ	After-tax value, determined by the buyer
V_S^τ	After-tax value, determined by the seller

Abbreviations

AETR	Accounting based effective tax rate
Art.	Article
AStG	Außensteuergesetz (German); Foreign Tax Act
BFH	Bundesfinanzhof (German); German Federal Tax Court
CCCTB	Common Consolidated Corporate Tax Base
CCCTB-PCD	Proposed Council Directive for a Common Consolidated Corporate Tax Base
CEX	Capital export neutrality
CFC	Controlled foreign corporations
CIN	Capital import neutrality
CPM	Cost-plus method
CUPM	Comparable uncontrolled price method
EBITDA	Earnings before interest, taxes, depreciation and amortization
EEA	European Economic Area
ECJ	European Court of Justice
e. g.	Exempli gratia (lat.); for example
EStG	Einkommensteuergesetz (German); German Income Tax Act
ETR	Effective tax rate
EU	European Union
FIFO	First-in-first-out
IAS	International Accounting Standard
i. e.	Id est (lat.); that is to say
IFRS	International Financial Reporting Standard
IP	Intellectual property
IRD	Interest and Royalties Directive
GAAP	Generally Accepted Accounting Principles
KStG	Körperschaftsteuergesetz (German); Corporation Tax Code
M&S	Marks & Spencer
MD	Merger Directive
No.	Number
NPV	Net present value
NPVT	Tax burden in net present value terms
OECD	Organization for Economic Co-operation and Development
OECD-MT	Model treaty of the Organization for Economic Co-operation and Development
p.	Page
Para.	Paragraph

PE	Permanent establishment
PSD	Parent Subsidiary Directive
R&D	Research and development
RPM	Resale price method
S.E.	Societas Europaea (lat.); European corporation
Sec.	Section
TC	Thin capitalization
TFEU	Treaty on the Functioning of the European Union
TNMM	Transactional net margin method
TPSM	Transactional profit split method
UK	United Kingdom
U.S.	United States
vs.	Versus

List of Tables

Table (1.1): Profit tax rates of corporations including local taxes (2011). Federal Ministry of Finance, 2012 7

1. International Company Taxation

1.1. Legal Structures of Company Taxation

1.1.1. Legally Distinct Entities

Taxpayers organize their economic activities in different legal forms, most notably sole proprietorships, partnerships and corporations. Civil law distinguishes between natural persons and legal persons. Sole proprietors are always natural persons, whereas the legal status of organizations depends on their corporate form. Partnerships, as a rule, have a limited legal personality. They can contract in the name of the partnership with third parties and the partners. The legal existence of a partnership may cease on a change of partners. By contrast, company law accords corporations full legal personality. A corporation, represented by its directors, can contract with third parties as well as with its own shareholders. The legal existence of a corporation is unaffected by a change in ownership of the shares. Some countries regard partnerships as companies with full legal personality (legal persons). Natural persons, partnerships and corporations may act as shareholders of corporations and partners of partnerships.

In general, tax law follows civil law, differentiating between natural persons and legal persons. Natural persons and legal persons are both taxable subjects. A corporation is taxable in its own right independently of its shareholders. Because the corporation is a legally distinct entity, its profit (taxable income) is subject to corporation tax. Corporate income is usually taxed at a proportional tax rate. If a corporation distributes its profits as dividends to its shareholders, those persons may be taxed on the dividends received.

Economic Double Taxation of Profits

Distributed after-tax corporate profits (dividends) are subject to individual income tax if the shareholder is a natural person. In effect, dividends are burdened with corporation tax and with individual income tax. From a legal perspective, two taxpayers (the corporation and the shareholder) are separately taxed, whilst from an economic perspective, the dividend is taxed twice. Therefore corporate profits suffer from economic double taxation. The extent to which economic double taxation of corporate profits is mitigated (or even completely eliminated) depends on the corporation tax system. Many countries, among them Germany, grant shareholder relief by partly exempting dividend income or by reducing the tax rate to which it is charged.

Example (1.1): The natural person P owns a 100% shareholding in C Corporation. P provides 1,000 equity capital to C Corporation, which earns a profit of 100. At a corporation tax rate of 40%, C Corporation's after-tax profit amounts to 60. C Corporation distributes its profit of 60 to P. The dividend received by P is included in P's taxable income and taxed at P's individual income tax rate of 40%. In order to reduce economic double taxation, P is allowed to deduct 50% of the dividend from his taxable income (i.e. an amount of 30 is treated as tax-free income). Thus, P's income tax burden with respect to the dividend amounts to 12 (= 30 · 40%). The total tax burden on the corporate profit of 100 amounts to 52 (= 40 + 12).

The corporation's shareholders are not taxed on the corporation's profit as long as the corporation retains its profits. If the profits are not distributed, corporate income is sheltered from an income tax charge on the shareholder. Instead of receiving a dividend, the shareholders may sell shares in the corporation, making a profit on the sale because the buyer pays for the corporation's retained profits. Capital gains upon the sale of shares usually trigger income taxes as well. As a result, the corporation`s profit is again taxed twice.

Losses of the corporation cannot be transferred to the shareholders for tax purposes. Losses may reduce the tax base of the corporation tax, but these losses do not result in individual income tax savings for the shareholders. Losses suffered by a corporation may be reflected in declining share prices. Shareholders may be allowed to write down the book value of shares held or to deduct a capital loss upon their sale.

Shareholder Contracts

Contracts concluded by corporations and their shareholders under civil law are accepted for tax purposes. Shareholders, therefore, may conclude a loan contract and provide debt capital to the corporation. The corporation is allowed to deduct interest payments from taxable income. The shareholders must include these corresponding interest payments in their own taxable income. In cases of shareholder debt financing, as opposed to equity financing, economic double taxation does not occur.

Example (1.2): Consider a shareholder loan substituting equity capital of 1,000 and assume an interest rate of 10%. The corporation earns a profit before interest payments of 100 and owes interest of 100, which reduces C Corporation's taxable income and the corporation tax to zero. P includes the interest payments received into its taxable income and pays an amount of 40 in individual income tax. Substituting equity financing with debt financing saves corporation tax of 40 and leads to additional individual income tax of 28 (= 40 – 12). The total tax savings due to debt financing amount to 12 (= 52 – 40).

Other shareholder contracts (e.g. lease contracts) may have the same effect. The payment of the corporation reduces both the corporation´s profit and the corporation tax, whereas the shareholders are taxed on the payment received. In order to protect the corporation tax revenue, the deductibility of payments relating to shareholder contracts is usually restricted in amount.

1.1.2. Pass-Through Entities

The profits earned by natural persons conducting business as sole proprietors are part of the taxable income and thus are burdened with individual income tax. In most countries, the tax schedule of the individual income tax is progressive, i.e. both the average tax rate and the marginal tax rate increase with increasing taxable income.

In countries where partnerships have a limited tax legal personality, the partnership is not regarded as a taxable subject. Partnerships are pass-through (transparent) entities, that is, their profits are allocated to the owners in the agreed ratio. Each owner (partner) pays taxes on his own profit share as part of his own income. As a result, the partners share in the partnerships profit is burdened with income tax. From this perspective, sole proprietors and natural persons as partners of a partnership are taxed in the same way. These taxpayers face the progressive income tax scale.[1]

No Economic Double Taxation of Profits

Business profits increase the taxable income of the owners or partners; losses can be deducted from their taxable income. If the partners are natural persons, profits and losses affect their individual income tax. If they are corporations, profits and losses affect the corporation income tax. Because profits and losses are only taxed once, economic double taxation does not occur.

Partner Contracts

Sole proprietors are not able to conclude contracts with their firm for civil law reasons. Partnerships, however, at least to a certain extent, may be regarded as legal entities under civil law. Consequently, partnerships are able to conclude contracts with their partners, e.g. for a loan. Although interest payments to partners reduce the partnership profit, their receipt may rank as partnership income under income tax law. Thus, partners and sole proprietors are effectively treated the same way for individual income tax purposes.

Example (1.3): A and B are partners of A & Co., a general partnership. Both partners hold 50% of the partnership´s capital. A & Co. earns a profit of 200. The partners´ taxable income is determined according to their share in the partnership's profit and thus amounts to 100 for each (= 50% · 200). If A and B both grant a loan of 1,000 to A & Co. at 10% interest, an amount of 100 will be due to each. The interest payments reduce the partnership's

---

1 In Germany, sole proprietors and partners of a partnership have the option to be taxed on retained profits at a reduced proportional tax rate and are taxed again when the profit is withdrawn (Sec. 34a Individual Income Tax Act, EStG).

profit to zero (= 200 – 200). A's as well as B's taxable income consists of the profit share of zero plus the interest payment of 100.

Partners in a partnership do not save income taxes when switching from partnership capital to loan capital if both profits and interest payments are taxed at the partner's individual income tax rate.

In general, the income tax position of the partners does not change if the partners switch from contributing equity capital to the partnership to funding it under a contractual agreement. The partners might, for example, lease assets to the partnership rather than paying in additional capital. Lease payments to the partners reduce the partnership's profit, but do not affect their taxable business income as the lease payment is added to their profit share.

1.2. Corporation Tax

1.2.1. Corporation Tax Base

Business profits are determined by accrual accounting. Accrual accounting is based on recording income when earned and expense when incurred in contrast to cash accounting which records the transactions when paid. The corporation's taxable income (profit or loss) is the net surplus of revenue over expense (net principle) based on accrual accounting. All revenues are taxable and all expenses are tax-deductible unless the tax law exempts revenues from the tax base or disallows specific expenses.

Business profits are taxed when income is realized (realization principle). Income is realized when a market transaction takes place, i.e. when assets are sold or services are provided to a third party. Consequently, all assets and liabilities are individually recognized in the balance sheet. Assets and liabilities are valued either at acquisition costs or manufacturing costs. Fixed assets with a useful life of more than one year are depreciated on the basis of historical cost over their expected useful life. By referring to market transactions, the realization principle ensures that taxpayers have sufficient liquid funds to settle their tax liability.

Taxable profits are usually determined by reference to the respective national Generally Accepted Accounting Principles (GAAP), subject to specific tax adjustments.[2] As both national GAAP and tax adjustments differ from country to country, national tax bases vary widely.

Depreciation

All countries taxing business profits allow the depreciation of fixed assets. However, the methods vary widely by country. Some countries, among them Germany, exclusively accept the straight-line depreciation method. Under the straight-line

2 In Germany, taxable profit is based on the legal financial statements (Sec. 5 Income Tax Act, EStG).

depreciation method, the amount of depreciation which can be deducted in a fiscal year is calculated by dividing the acquisition or manufacturing cost of an asset by the number of years of its expected useful life.

Many countries, among them France, allow a choice between the straight-line and declining-balance depreciation methods. Under the declining-balance method, the amount of depreciation which can be deducted in a fiscal year is calculated by applying the applicable depreciation rate to the book value of the asset. Declining-balance depreciation is usually restricted in amount by a maximum depreciation rate.

Most countries depreciate single assets, whereas some countries, among them the UK, apply the declining-balance method on a pool basis. All assets acquired in a fiscal year are added to the pool on the basis of their acquisition cost. The value of the pool is multiplied by the applicable depreciation rate to calculate the depreciation amount deductible for tax purposes.

Goodwill

The differences in tax accounting rules may also be illustrated by the example of goodwill. Goodwill is defined as the market value of the firm's equity capital less the current book value of net assets as calculated for tax purposes. As a rule, and in all Member States of the EU, self-created goodwill is not to be capitalized for tax purposes. All expenses relating to self-created goodwill are immediately deducted from the tax base.

By contrast, acquired goodwill is created by a market transaction, where all assets and liabilities of a business are acquired (asset deal). The acquired goodwill is defined as acquisition cost (acquisition price of the acquired net assets) less the current value of the net assets in the balance sheet. Acquired goodwill must usually be capitalized and depreciated for tax purposes. The useful life over which the goodwill is expensed (regularly straight-line) differs widely. Within the EU, useful life ranges from five years in Belgium to 20 years in Spain. In some countries, regular depreciation is not allowed at all, e.g. in the United Kingdom.

Deductibility of Expenses

The net principle in connection with corporate taxation implies that many payments from corporations to shareholders are tax-deductible. The most important examples are salaries, rental payments, interest payments and royalties relating to services or capital the shareholders provide to the corporation. In all countries, certain expenses may not be deductible for tax purposes. The most prominent examples are fines and corporation taxes. Profit distributions are usually not deductible as expense and are thus burdened with corporation taxes.

The deductibility of expenses offers scope for tax planning. Corporations have an incentive to transfer profits to the shareholders via contracts generating deductible expenses instead of paying non-deductible dividends. In consequence, tax law restrictions prevent corporations from excessively reducing their tax base in this way. Transactions between corporations and shareholders must be at arm´s length.

This arm's length principle demands that the conditions stipulated in the contracts between shareholders and corporations are comparable to conditions to which unrelated parties would have agreed in similar circumstances. A shareholder loan, for example, is not at arm's length, if the interest rate stipulated in the loan contract would not have been accepted by third parties. Expenses which are not at arm's length are not deductible from the corporation tax base and may be classified as profit distributions.

Loss Deduction

In the event of an overall corporate loss, an immediate tax refund is not usually available. Losses which cannot be deducted in the year of assessment may be carried back or carried forward. Loss carry-forward and loss carry-back ensure that all expenses relating to business income can be deducted over time, which conforms to the net principle. In the EU, the loss offset is a common feature of all corporation tax systems. Still, loss deduction is very often restricted. A loss carry-back is only allowed in a few EU Member States and is sometimes restricted by amount and always by time. A loss carry-forward is offered by all EU Member States, but may be restricted by time or by amount. In all EU Member States, the loss carry-forward is not interest-bearing.

1.2.2. Corporation Tax Rates

As a general rule, corporation tax is charged at a single fixed rate. However, there may be special rates for low incomes or specific activities. In some countries, local taxes are levied in addition to corporation tax. Countries may levy a trade or business tax on business income, as does Germany. The rate of the German trade tax is determined by the uniform factor of 3.5% set in the federal Trade Tax Act and the local multiplier set by each local authority with trade tax entitlement. The minimum local multiplier is set in the Trade Tax Act at 200%. An average local multiplier can be taken at 400%, which gives an average trade tax rate of 14% (= 3.5% · 400%).

The one German corporation tax rate is 15%, plus the solidarity surcharge of 0.825% (5.5% of the corporation tax due). The average overall corporate profit tax burden in Germany is nearly 30% (=15.825% + 14%). However, this can rise to as much as nearly 33% where the local multiplier is 490% (e.g. in Munich). Note that the trade tax base includes items which are deductible for purposes of the corporation tax, e.g. only 75% of interest payments are tax-deductible for trade tax.

The corporation tax rates in the EU range from 10% in Bulgaria and Cyprus to 35% in Malta (as of 2011). The tax rates in the eastern EU Member States are usually lower than those in the western EU Member States. An exception is Ireland with a corporation tax rate of 12.5%. Table (1.1) displays the tax burdens charged to corporate profits (including local profits taxes) in 2011.

Table (1.1): Tax burden on corporate profits including local taxes (2011). Federal Ministry of Finance, 2012.

Country	Tax Burden %
Bulgaria	10.00
Cyprus	10.00
Ireland	12.50
Latvia	15.00
Lithuania	15.00
Romania	16.00
Poland	19.00
Slovakia	19.00
Czech Republic	19.00
Slovenia	20.00
Hungary	20.62
Estonia	21.00
Greece	24.00
Denmark	25.00
Netherlands	25.00
Austria	25.00
Finland	26.00
UK	26.00
Sweden	26.30
Portugal	26.50
Canada	28.00
Luxembourg	28.80
Germany	29.83
Spain	30.00
Italy	31.40
Belgium	33.99
France	34.43
Malta	35.00
Japan	39.55
U.S.A.	39.62

In 2011, the average corporate tax burdens in the EU amounts to 23.80%.[3] In the OECD countries it was 26% (as of 2011).[4]

1.2.3. Corporation Tax System

Corporate profits are taxed twice whereas profits of partnerships (and sole proprietors) are only taxed once. Most income tax systems address economic double taxation of corporate profits at the shareholder level.

Withholding Tax

The shareholders of a corporation are taxed on the dividend by means of a withholding tax deducted from the gross dividend paid. The tax is collected from the corporation. The corporation is obliged to withhold the tax on behalf of the shareholders and to forward the tax revenue to the taxing authority. Sometimes this tax is a final burden, leaving the shareholders with no further obligations in this regard. If it is not, the amount withheld can be credited against the shareholders′ income tax due on the dividend. An excess of withholding tax may be refundable.

Shareholder Taxation

If corporate shareholders qualify for the affiliation privilege, their dividends received are tax-free. The affiliation privilege prevents inter-corporate dividends from being taxed twice and avoids economic double taxation of dividends as long as the profits do not leave the corporate sphere. In Germany all inter-corporate dividends are exempt from corporation tax, although 5% of the amount is disallowed as a deductible expense. As a result, 95% of the dividends are tax-free. Withholding taxes are refunded to the corporate shareholders.

Natural person shareholders suffer a further income tax charge on their dividend income. This is in addition to the corporation tax already borne. The corporation tax burden on dividends can be taken into account to avoid, or at least mitigate, economic double taxation. The tax burden of distributed corporate profits depends on both the corporation and the individual income tax. The corporation tax system determines how the corporation tax is integrated into individual income taxation.

With respect to the integration of corporation taxation into the individual income taxation, three systems can be discerned: (i) Classical systems with full double taxation. Corporate profits and the distributed dividends are fully taxed twice. (ii) Double taxation avoidance systems where taxes are either levied on the corporations or on the shareholders. In the latter case, the corporation taxes levied on dividends are refunded. (iii) Double taxation mitigation systems with taxes on both levels with some relief for the shareholders.

---

3 van Boeijen-Ostaszewska, Ola; Schellekens, Marnix (2012).

4 van Boeijen-Ostaszewska, Ola; Schellekens, Marnix (2012).

Within the EU, double taxation is avoided or mitigated at the shareholder level. Most Member States reduce either the amount of taxable dividends or the tax rate which applies to dividends received by natural persons (shareholder relief).

Shareholder Relief System

Under the shareholder relief system, the corporation tax is not fully integrated into the individual income tax as would be necessary to avoid double taxation entirely. Thus, double taxation of corporate profits from the charge of both corporation and income tax is only mitigated.

Example (1.4): P Corporation is a resident of country P and earns a profit (before taxes) of 100, which is burdened with 25% corporation tax. The profit after taxes is distributed to domestic shareholders (natural persons). Upon distribution, the shareholders are subject to a withholding tax (20%), which is an income tax on the dividend paid by the corporation on behalf of the shareholders. The shareholders receive the net profit after corporation tax and withholding tax. The withholding tax is credited against the income tax liability of the shareholders. The tax law of country P stipulates that only 50% of gross dividends received are subject to individual income tax (relief at the tax base). The shareholders` income tax rate is 40%.

1	Profit before taxes		100.00
2	Corporation tax	25% · (1)	25.00
3	Profit after taxes (dividend)	(1) – (2)	75.00
4	Withholding tax	20% · (3)	15.00
5	Gross dividend received	(3)	75.00
6	Taxable income - shareholders	50% · (5)	37.50
7	Income tax	40% · (6)	15.00
8	Withholding tax credit	(4)	15.00
9	Income tax payment	(7) – (8)	0.00
10	Net income of shareholders	(5) – (4) – (9)	60.00
11	Tax burden on distributed profits	(2) + (4) + (9)	40.00

In this example, the overall tax rate of 40% [= 25% + 50% · 40% · (1 – 25%)] equals the individual income tax rate of 40%. For all other individual income tax rates, this is not the case.

The tax burden on corporate profits depends on the design of the shareholder relief system. In Germany, in case of private shareholdings, there is a reduced income tax rate of 26.38% (25% plus 5.5% solidarity surcharge). However, income from business shareholdings of natural persons is 40% tax-free. Given the individual income tax rate τ (including solidarity surcharge), relief at the tax base and at the tax rate are equivalent if $1 - 0.6 \cdot \tau = 1 - 0.2638$ which gives $\tau = 43.96\%$. A tax burden of 43.96% is close to the top income tax rate of 47.48% (including solidarity surcharge).

1.2.4. Group Taxation

The tax law of all countries respects corporations as entities which are legally distinct from their shareholders. Yet, in many countries special tax rules apply to groups of corporations. Under group taxation rules, the income of the group is taxed in total instead of the income of each member of the group individually. Group taxation rules address the problem that losses incurred by a corporation cannot be transferred to the shareholders. Group taxation rules allow the group to transfer a loss from a group company suffering the loss to another group company earning a profit. To the extent that transferred losses are absorbed by profits, the group enjoys an immediate loss offset.

Requirements of Group Taxation Regimes

Most group taxation regimes are restricted to group companies which are located in the same country as the parent company. Foreign group companies are usually excluded from the tax group. Group taxation requirements are aimed at centrally controlled groups with a common business objective. In general, group taxation is available if two conditions concerning the tax residence of group members and the shareholding are met: (i) the affiliate companies are domestic corporations owned by a domestic parent, (ii) the subsidiaries are controlled by the parent. As rule, control is assumed if the shareholding exceeds 50% or 75%.

Group Taxation Regimes

Group taxation comes in many different forms. Few countries offer full consolidation of intra-group profits and losses along the lines of financial accounting and treating the group as a single unit. Most countries have implemented group taxation regimes which do not completely overlook the fact that corporations are legally distinct entities. These group taxation schemes are based on the transfer of taxable income from one group member to another. Basically, the following systems of group taxation can be identified.

Aggregation, Group Relief, Group Contribution

Aggregation systems separately compute corporate income of each member of the group and then add the results to a group total. Usually, the parent company which is entitled to receive the profits and has to absorb the losses is liable to pay the tax. Some countries (e.g. Denmark and France) allow worldwide aggregation. Under a group relief system (e.g. UK), losses are transferred within the group. As a rule, loss transfer can take place upward (subsidiary to parent), sideways (subsidiary to subsidiary) and downward (parent to subsidiary). The transferor loses the right to a future loss offset, whereas the transferee can deduct the loss immediately from its profit. The group contribution system (e.g. Finland and Sweden) allows profits to be transferred within the group by payments. The transfer can be upward, sideways and downwards. The transferring company can deduct the payment as business expense, whereas the transferee has to include it in its taxable income. As a result, the loss is deducted from the profits of the transferor.

Aggregation systems, group relief system and group contribution system do not fully consolidate the group's profits and losses. Thus, profits or losses from intra-group transactions are not eliminated from the tax base. Rollover relief, i.e. the tax free transfer of an asset within the group at tax book value, may be available for some assets, but it is almost always restricted to the domestic part of the group.

Full Consolidation

Full tax consolidation systems (e.g. the Netherlands) seek to tax the domestic group as a single economic unit. Intra-group transactions are disregarded for tax purposes. As result, loss compensation is effected and profits from intra-group transactions are eliminated from the tax base. Apportionment of the consolidated group income to the region in which it was earned may be on the basis of a formula (e.g. as in U.S. state taxation).

This brief survey of group taxation schemes shows that group taxation can either be based on the transfer of wealth (aggregation and group contribution) or on the mere transfer of taxable income within the group (group relief and full consolidation).

1.3. International Double Taxation

1.3.1. Limited and Unlimited Tax Liability

Countries levy taxes on the income of residents (legal and natural persons) and on the income of non-residents. Accordingly, there are two different forms of tax liability: unlimited tax liability and limited tax liability.

Unlimited Tax Liability

Unlimited tax liability applies to natural persons, who are residents of a country. Legal persons, in particular corporations, are subject to unlimited tax liability in the country where their legal seat (registered office) or place of effective management is located (residence country). Corporate and individual taxpayers subject to unlimited tax liability are taxed on their worldwide income (worldwide income principle).[5]

Limited Tax Liability

Limited tax liability applies to legal persons and natural persons who are not residents but perform certain economic activities in the country (source country). Corporate and individual taxpayers subject to limited tax liability are taxed on their income derived in the territory of the source country (territorial income principle).

In the field of business taxation, limited tax liability applies to business activities performed through a branch without own legal personality. If a corporation performs economic activities in a foreign country through a branch, it is subject to limited corporation tax liability. If natural persons (e.g., a sole proprietor) perform business activities in a foreign country through a branch, their income is subject to limited individual income tax liability. Only the profits attributed to the branch are subject to tax in the source country.

In case of dividend payments, license payments or interest payments which have their origin in the source country (e.g. a subsidiary located in the source country makes the payments), the source country may establish limited tax liability of the recipient of this income and levy a withholding tax on the gross payments.

Exports are usually not covered by territorial income taxation, because there is (in tax terms) no connection with the territory of the foreign country. However, if the exporter establishes a taxable link to the foreign country through a branch, profits attributable to the exports may be taxed.

1.3.2. Legal Double Taxation

Investors suffer from legal double taxation if they are subject to both limited and unlimited tax liability. More precisely, legal double taxation occurs if two sovereign countries levy a comparable tax on the same taxable object of the same taxable entity within the same period of time. Taxpayers investing in the source country through a branch are taxed on the branch's profits in the source country (limited tax liability) and in the country of residence (unlimited tax liability). Taxpayers receiving payments in the source country may be taxed on the payments received. The residence country will include the gross payments into the (world-

[5] Exceptions to the worldwide income principle are rare. In France, for example, corporations are taxed on their domestic income only.

wide) income of the recipients and levy income tax on their income under unlimited tax liability.

With respect to the withholding tax the source country may levy on dividends, the shareholders suffer from legal double taxation. Economic double taxation, by contrast to legal double taxation, refers to different taxpayers (shareholder and corporation) who are together taxed twice on the same taxable object (the corporation's profit) by one or more tax authorities.

Other Reasons for Legal Double Taxation

The coexistence of unlimited and limited tax liability is not the only reason for legal double taxation. Legal double taxation can also occur in cases of double unlimited tax liability due to double residence. If, for example, a corporation has its legal seat (place of incorporation) in Germany and its place of management in Great Britain, the corporation is subject to unlimited tax liability in both countries. Double limited tax liability is another reason for double taxation. If, for example, a Polish branch of a German corporation receives dividends from a U.S. subsidiary, the German corporation is subject to limited tax liability in the U.S. and in Poland with respect to the dividends received, because these dividends are included in the Polish branch's profit. Overlapping tax bases due to conflicting determination of taxable income may also cause double taxation. For example, the U.S. rules to determine the profit of a German branch may differ from the respective German rules.

Measures to Avoid Legal Double Taxation

National income tax law aims at reducing or avoiding legal double taxation. In addition, countries conclude bilateral tax treaties on double taxation. A double tax treaty is international law and ranks higher than national law. The treaty does not establish taxing rights, but allocates existing taxing rights to the contracting countries. The tax allocation rules of a double tax treaty restrict the taxing right of the source country and oblige the residence country to reduce its tax claim to eliminate any legal double taxation.

The contracting countries have agreed to avoid double taxation. Yet, the taxpayers have no legal claim to the elimination of double taxation. In cases of conflicting tax liability, double taxation can be avoided or mitigated by the country of residence or the country of source. If according to the provisions of the contracting countries′ national law, taxpayers are resident in both countries (e.g. if a corporation's seat and place of effective management differ) the tax treaty's so-called tie-breaker rule applies. The tie-breaker rule allocates the taxing right to one of the contracting parties (in the above example to the country where the corporation's place of effective management is situated). As regards the double taxation due to overlapping tax bases, the tax treaties explicitly address the problem in cases of intra-group transactions.

Germany has signed a double tax treaty with every EU Member State and many other non-EU countries. Altogether, Germany has concluded more than 90 double tax treaties with countries all over the world (as of 2011).

1.3.3. OECD Model Treaty

Most double taxation treaties are based on the model treaty of the OECD.[6] They follow the structure and often the wording of the OECD model treaty (OECD-MT). However, the OECD-MT is not legally binding. Its main purpose is to give guidance to tax treaty negotiators when concluding their own treaties. In this sense, the OECD-MT functions as the basis for most double tax treaties.

Two fundamental principles govern the OECD-MT. The taxing right of the source country is acknowledged, but may be restricted. The taxing right of the residence country is confirmed, but is conditional on the obligation to eliminate possible double taxation.

Source Country

Regarding the source country, three categories can be discerned with respect to the extent of the taxing right. The source country's taxing right can be unlimited, restricted or non-existent.

An unlimited taxing right of the source country is granted for real property (Art. 6 OECD-MT) and for profits of permanent establishments located there (Art. 5 and Art. 7 OECD-MT). The tax legal term "permanent establishment" includes especially a place of management, a branch, an office or a factory. Facilities, however, which serve the sole purpose of storage, display or delivery of goods, are not regarded as "permanent establishment".

The taxing right of the source country is restricted for dividends paid by a resident company to non-residents (Art. 10 OECD-MT). A withholding tax rate up to 5% of the gross amount is allowed if the shareholding exceeds 25% and is held by a corporation; a withholding tax rate up to 15% of the gross amount is allowed in all other cases. Furthermore, the source country´s taxing right is restricted for interest paid by a resident company to non-residents (Art. 11 OECD-MT). A withholding tax rate up to 10% of the gross amount is allowed.

The source country has no taxing right for royalties paid to non-residents (Art. 12 OECD-MT) and capital gains on shareholdings of non-residents in resident corporations (Art. 13 OECD-MT).

Residence Country

The residence country has the right to tax worldwide income of resident taxpayers who are liable to tax by reason of domicile, residence, place of management or similar criteria. If a taxpayer is resident in both countries, tie-breaker rules deter-

---

6 See OECD Model Tax Convention on Income and Capital (2010).

mine the tax residence (Art. 4 OECD-MT). Business profits are taxed in the state of residence of a company unless the profits are attributable to a permanent establishment in the source country (Art. 7 OECD-MT). The residence country avoids legal double taxation by granting relief for taxes paid in the source country, if the source country exercises its taxing right.

The OECD-MT offers the exemption method (Art. 23A OECD-MT) and the credit method (Art. 23B OECD-MT). The contracting countries are free to choose between the two. The country of residence may avoid legal double taxation by exempting the foreign income from its tax base, or by crediting the foreign taxes paid. In any case, these measures only aim at avoiding legal double taxation; they do not address economic double taxation.

Exemption Method

Under the exemption method, the country of residence exempts foreign income from the domestic tax base. Only the source country taxes the income. The tax burden is determined by the tax rate and the tax base of the source country. Foreign losses are relieved in the foreign country. The residence country forgoes tax revenue related to the foreign income but does not relieve foreign losses. Exemption may be conditional on subject to tax clauses (foreign income must be burdened with foreign taxes) or activity clauses (foreign income must be derived from activities which are not seen as tax avoidance activities or as otherwise undesirable). German tax treaties, as a rule, grant exemption for real property, business profits and income of the self-employed.

Double tax treaties may exempt foreign dividends received by a resident corporation, subject to minimum shareholding requirements (international affiliation privilege). The international affiliation privilege is ineffective if the corporation tax law of a contracting country exempts foreign dividends from the tax base. Indeed, corporation tax law often grants unconditional exemption of all kinds of dividends. For example, all dividends received by a German corporation are tax-free under national law (5% of the dividend is deemed to be a non-deductible business expense and therefore are subject to tax).

The exemption method is widely applied by the Member States of the EU. There seems to be a tendency towards the application of the exemption method. One reason may be that compliance and enforcement costs are supposedly low when foreign income is exempted from domestic taxation. Another reason may be that the exemption method leads to a level playing field for domestic firms investing in foreign countries because all investors face the same tax burden in the respective foreign market.

Credit Method

Under the credit method, foreign income is included in the domestic tax base. The foreign income tax paid on foreign income is credited against the domestic income tax due on that foreign income. As a result, the tax revenue is shared between the source country and the residence country. Some countries apply the credit method consistently in national tax law and in double tax treaties (e.g. the U.S.). Germany relies on the credit method in national tax law, but restricts it in double taxation treaties to dividends and to interest income.

The foreign tax credit applies to the foreign income tax due on the same income of the same taxpayer in the same period as the domestic income tax. The foreign tax has to be comparable in nature to the domestic income tax. Taxes on different persons are not comparable to the income tax of the domestic taxpayer. Foreign corporation income tax on profits, in particular, cannot be credited against the domestic individual income tax on the dividends received from those profits. On the other hand, a country's corporation tax system may allow foreign corporation tax to be credited against the domestic corporation tax on taxable dividends.

The tax credit is limited to the lesser of the amount of foreign taxes paid and the amount of domestic taxes due on the foreign income (ordinary credit). Additional domestic taxation arises if the foreign taxes are lower than the domestic taxes. If the foreign taxes are higher, the residence country does not refund the difference between foreign taxes and domestic taxes (excess credit). From a fiscal point of view, a tax refund is unacceptable as it be a tax revenue transfer to a foreign jurisdiction.[7] As a result, foreign income is effectively exempted if foreign income taxes are higher than domestic income taxes.

On the worldwide income principle, foreign losses as well as foreign profits are included in the domestic income. However, the tax law in the source country may give the taxpayer the right to carry forward the loss locally. If there is a loss offset in the source country, the inclusion of the foreign loss in the worldwide income seems to lead to relieving the loss twice. Ultimately, though this is not the case because the loss carry forward reduces the creditable foreign tax thus increasing domestic taxes due.

Example (1.5): A sole proprietor suffers from a loss of 50 in the source country in year 1 and earns a profit of 50 in year 2. The loss carry forward is fully effective in the source country in year 2. As a result, the foreign country does not collect income taxes in year 1 and in year 2. The foreign loss of 50 is fully claimed in the sole proprietor's residence country in year 1 and reduces domestic income taxes. In year 2 the foreign profit of 50 increases the taxable income and the income taxes of the sole proprietor. Due to the loss carry forward, taxes are not paid in the source country and, thus, not credited in the country of residence. As a result, the foreign loss has effectively been deducted only once.

Restrictions on the foreign tax credit are common. All restrictions aim at limiting the pooling of highly taxed and lightly taxed foreign income. In Germany, the tax credit is limited on a per country basis (per country limitation). Per country limitation prevents pooling of excess with unused credits. In the U.S. for example the restrictions on the tax credit apply to pooling income by type (income basket-limitation).

---

7 Note that a tax refund generates an incentive for the foreign country to increase its taxes. Foreign investors do not suffer from an additional tax burden if their country of residence refunds the foreign tax increase.

1.4. International Profit Allocation

1.4.1. Transfer Pricing

1.4.1.1. Market Prices

Multinational companies invest in several countries through legally distinct corporations (subsidiaries) or legally dependent branches (permanent establishments). Each subsidiary or branch which is a part of the multinational company is taxed on the basis of its share in the multinational company's total profit. The countries tax the profits attributed to subsidiaries and permanent establishments based on unlimited tax liability (subsidiary) or based on limited tax liability (permanent establishment). In either case, the overall profit of a multinational company has to be apportioned to the countries where its subsidiaries or permanent establishments are located.

Arm's Length Principle

The dealing at arm's length principle is the corner stone of international profit allocation. Conditions made or imposed between associated parties in their commercial or financial relations (controlled transactions) are not supposed to differ from those which would have been agreed upon by independent parties (uncontrolled transactions). Transfer prices have to be adjusted for tax purposes, if contract conditions are such that the contract would not have been signed by independent parties. Stipulated prices have to be compared to market prices for the goods transferred or the services provided. If the transfer price differs from the market price, the taxpayer's income has to be adjusted on the basis of the market price.

Shortcomings of the Arm's Length Principle

The key assumption behind the dealing at arm's length principle is the comparability of controlled transactions with uncontrolled transactions. At first glance, the dealing at arm's length principle is an economically convincing concept. Transfer prices are judged on the basis of market prices of comparable transactions which are not controlled by the taxpayer. However, the idea of comparability disregards the essence of an integrated firm. Acting as an economic entity means exploiting the competitive advantages of being integrated. In the case of an internal transaction, the firm has rejected market coordination and has decided to rely on hierarchy as a means of coordinating transactions.[8] The concept of comparability implies that another firm facing the same economic circumstances uses market coordination. But given economic reasons for internal coordination, all comparable firms reject market coordination. From a theoretical point of view, under these

8 See Coase (1937) and Williamson (1985).

circumstances, market prices of comparable uncontrolled transactions are non-existent.

Because the domestic company and the foreign subsidiary form an economic unit, most goods transferred and services provided are firm-specific and, thus, not traded by independent parties in markets. Assume a foreign subsidiary produces a product based on research and development activities, undertaken by the domestic parent. Based on a license agreement, the foreign subsidiary pays the stipulated price (transfer price) to the parent for the know-how transferred. Under the arm's length principle, the transfer price for the know-how should conform to the market price of a comparable transaction. However, because know-how is a firm-specific asset which is not traded on the market, a market price cannot be established.

From an economic point of view, the allocation of a multinational company's total profit to the countries where the company invests is essentially unclear. To grasp this fundamental problem, assume a multinational company which has located research and development in Country A and production in Country B, whereas the finished products are sold to customers at a total profit in Country C. For tax purposes, the total profit has to be allocated to the functions performed in the three countries. Yet, it is impossible to allocate the group's total profit fairly according to economic functions performed or input factors involved in the production of the goods sold. Yet, international profit allocation is fundamental for national taxation. Income tax law must ignore the fact that a multinational company consisting of several corporations and branches acts as an economic unit and that it is impossible to correctly split up the company's total profit.

1.4.1.2. Subsidiary

Corporation tax law follows separate entity accounting, taking into account the market transactions (purchases and sales) of a corporation. Separate entity accounting applies also to internal transactions of the multinational company. Affiliated corporations are legally distinct entities and may enter into legal contracts which are in principal accepted by tax law. To determine the profit of a subsidiary, internal transactions are accounted for on the basis of transfer prices stipulated in legal contracts. For tax purposes, transfer prices have to conform to the arm's length standard (Art. 9 Para. 1 OECD-MT) implying a comparison of the transfer price to the market price of a comparable transaction.

Because market prices for international transactions rarely exist, multinational companies experience an incentive to make use of the imprecision of transfer pricing to reduce their overall tax burden. On the other hand, a multinational company may face double taxation due to overlapping tax bases if the transfer pricing rules applied by the countries involved do not correspond. Tax administrations are aware of profit shifting opportunities and impose strict rules and extensive documentation requirements on the multinational companies to limit their room for maneuver. As a result, the companies' cost of compliance with the tax law increases as does the tax administration´s cost to apply the law and to collect taxes.

If market prices cannot be directly established, the OECD Transfer Pricing Guidelines[9] accept different methods to assess the arm's length price. The Transfer Pricing Guidelines describe three standard methods.

Standard Methods

The comparable uncontrolled price method (CUPM) compares prices charged in controlled transactions (within the group) to prices charged in uncontrolled transactions between independent enterprises. CUPM is closest to the idea behind the dealing at arm's length principle because it is directly related to market prices which are charged in transactions of independent parties or by the company in transactions with third parties. CUPM is in particular appropriate for trading firms.

The cost-plus method (CPM) determines the transfer price on the basis of direct and indirect production costs plus a profit margin. CPM is the standard method with the widest range of application because it is not directly related to market prices. CPM is a particularly appropriate method for industrial companies.

The resale price method (RPM) determines the transfer price by deducting a gross profit margin from the price the reseller charges to third parties. The gross profit margin compensates the resellers for the functions they perform and the risk they bear. As opposed to CPM, RPM relies on market prices of the goods transferred. RPM is in particular suited for distributors.

Profit Based Methods

Apart from the three standard methods, the OECD Transfer Pricing Guidelines allow the transactional net margin method (TNMM). TNMM allocates profit to transactions according to a certain business ratio. Such a ratio could be the sales profitability (ratio of profit to sales), which can be seen in uncontrolled transactions. TNMM focuses on net profit indicators, whereas RPM and CPM are based on gross margins. Net profit indicators may be less responsive to functional differences between controlled and uncontrolled transactions. CPM, RPM and TNMM have in common that margins in a controlled transaction are assessed by comparison with respective margins of a comparable uncontrolled transaction.

CPM, RPM and TNMM consider information of only one transaction party. For instance, RPM is applied if activities of the sales department are insignificant and can easily be observed whereas the production process is complex. If, by contrast, costs can be easily computed and the reseller does substantially contribute to the value of the product, then CPM is selected. Choosing one of these methods allows abstracting from information which is difficult to obtain or even unavailable. Nevertheless, assessing the remunerations and margins of firm-specific transactions can be very controversial.

---

[9] See OECD Transfer Pricing Guidelines (2010).

A one-sided approach to determine transfer prices is inappropriate if each party to a transaction makes valuable and unique contributions and if both parties perform a multitude of functions. In situations where transactions are highly integrated, the transactional profit split method (TPSM) comes into play. If intra-firm transactions are closely linked an appropriate transfer price can only be determined if transactions of integrated processes are combined. The total profit from a controlled transaction is identified and split up among the parties involved. Profits are divided in relation to profits which unrelated enterprises would expect in comparable transactions.

The usual methods to split up the profits are contribution analysis or residual analysis. While contribution analysis splits up the combined profits according to a controlled transaction based on the allocation of functions and risks, the residual analysis divides the combined profits into two stages. First, each party gets an arm's length remuneration for its non-unique contributions in relation to the controlled transaction in which it is engaged. This remuneration can be determined by applying CUPM, RPM, CPM or TNMM. Second, any remaining residual profit is allocated among the parties involved based on an analysis of the facts and circumstances of the controlled transaction. In practice, the division of the combined profits is generally achieved by allocation keys.

Example (1.6): A subsidiary produces and sells optical devices under license from the parent. The subsidiary incurs production costs of 100, pays a license fee of 130 to the parent and has revenues of 250 from the sale of the products to third parties. Under the TPSM, the profit of 150, calculated before the license fee is deducted, can be split into two parts. The subsidiary performs a production function which is rewarded by the imputed market rate of return on the employed capital. Assume a market return of 20. Then, the residual profit of 130 (=150 – 20) has to be allocated to the parent company for providing the intangible which earns the economic yield of 130. The license fee of 130 is thus at arm's length.

TNMM and TPSM are appropriate in situations where none of the three standard methods can be reasonably applied. This is particularly the case when self-created intangible assets (like technical know-how or patents) are transferred or licensed. CUPM cannot be applied because market prices are not available. CPM is inapplicable because the cost of producing an intangible cannot be determined with any degree of accuracy. Moreover, the value of an intangible asset cannot be properly assessed by referring to production cost because it is dependent upon discounted future cash flows. TNMM is usually impossible because it lacks a comparable transaction to assess a profit margin.

1.4.1.3. Permanent Establishment

A permanent establishment is a fixed place of business through which the business is carried on. The country where the permanent establishment is located is entitled to tax the profits attributed to the permanent establishment (Art. 7 Para. 2 OECD-MT). The company's total profit must be attributed to the domestic and the foreign part of the company respectively following the dealing at arm‘s-length principle.

Because the foreign permanent establishment and the domestic parent company (the head office) are an economic unit as well as a legal unit (in the sense that the permanent establishment is not legally separate), it is impossible for the principal company to enter into legal contracts with the foreign permanent establishment. Thus, as opposed to legally separated subsidiaries, transfer prices stipulated in legal contracts governing the internal transactions are non-existent.

Indirect Method of Profit Allocation

A first solution to the problem of profit allocation in case of permanent establishments is provided by the so-called indirect method of profit allocation. This method uses allocation factors to allocate the total profit to a company's business units (formula allocation). Under the indirect method, the firm's total profit is allocated to the domestic and the foreign part of the business according to economic factors like capital, wages and sales. The rationale behind such an allocation rule is the idea that economic factors entering the apportionment formula are linked to actually earned profits. Capital and labor are production factors. Taking these factors into account, the company's profit is allocated to the countries where production takes place, i.e. where capital is invested and where wages are paid. Sales are connected to marketing activities. Taking sales into account, allocates a company's profit to countries where goods are delivered or services performed.

Although it seems to be plausible from an economic point of view to allocate a company's total profit according to factors that are related to production and sales, it is essentially unclear what amount of profit is "caused" by invested capital and employed workforce or generated revenues. We lack any economic theory how to allocate a firm's profit fairly according to the input factors involved. Profit allocation based on formula allocation is, thus, unfounded in economics.

Direct Method of Profit Allocation

In practice, the direct method is the standard method for profit allocation in the case of permanent establishments. The direct method rests on the assumption that the permanent establishment is economically independent for tax purposes (although it is legally dependent). The profits attributed to a permanent establishment are the profits the permanent establishment would earn if it were a separate and independent enterprise.

Under the OECD approach, a two-step analysis is required. Firstly, a functional analysis must be performed to identify functions performed, assets owned or used and risks assumed. The functional analysis identifies the economically significant activities performed by the permanent establishment. Secondly, the remuneration of dealings between the parent company and the permanent establishment is determined by assessing transfer prices used by legally separated entities (i.e. corporations).

Because the permanent establishment is deemed to be independent for the purpose of international profit allocation, the foreign permanent establishment can deduct expenses and account for revenues which relate to internal transactions. As a consequence, the permanent establishment may, for example, deduct interest payments for a loan granted by the principal company. If the principal company transfers goods (e.g. intermediate goods) to the permanent establishment, the principal company accounts for the revenues, while the permanent establishment deducts the corresponding expenses. Transfer prices have to be at arm's length in line with the rules of the OECD governing transfer prices in case of corporations, i.e. CUPM, CPM, RPM, TNMM, and TPSM apply accordingly. In effect, the permanent establishment is treated as a separate and independent enterprise only for purposes of profit attribution, which from a legal point of view is mere fiction.

1.4.2. Cross-border Reorganization

International profit allocation is not only necessary when assets are transferred in the course of normal business transactions. Assets may also leave a tax jurisdiction on the occasion of the restructuring of a business, e.g. when a domestic corporation is merged into a foreign corporation.

Tax computation is based on historical costs and the realization principle. Market prices which exceed an asset's tax book value (hidden reserves) do not of themselves give rise to a taxable profit. Taxable profit arises only in the event of a market transaction (realization). A taxpayer could exploit international tax rate divergences if assets were transferred at tax book value from one jurisdiction to another. In effect the taxpayer could choose where to pay taxes if transfers at tax book value were allowed. Therefore, hidden reserves are taxed upon the cross-border transfer of assets if otherwise a country would lose its tax claim (exit taxation). Exit taxation of hidden reserves prevents international tax rate arbitrage.

Yet, exit taxation may be a serious impediment to cross-border restructuring because profits are taxed before they are realized. As a result, a company may face high exit taxes without having access to liquid funds or additional debt to settle the tax claim. Efficiency gains from restructuring may not be reaped for tax reasons. Given these negative economic effects, exit taxation should be restricted to cases where exit taxation is necessary from a fiscal point of view.

Transfer of Seat

Corporations can leave a country by transferring their legal seat (registered office) or place of management to another country in order to benefit from lower corporation taxes. Because unlimited tax liability is linked to the legal seat or the place of management, corporations are no longer subject to domestic tax liability when they abandon their domestic tax residence. From a tax perspective, the corporations` assets leave the former state of residence and are transferred to the new. In principal, the new state of residence has the right to tax the profits stemming from the corporations` assets. Hidden reserves of transferred assets are realized in the foreign country upon the sale of the assets.

A departing corporation still may own business assets in the former country of residence. In case the respective assets qualify as a permanent establishment, the former country of residence has a tax claim on the profits of that permanent establishment in terms of the limited tax liability of the now non-resident (departed) corporation. Yet, valuable assets, such as goodwill or other intangibles, are usually allocated to the corporation's new foreign headquarter for tax purposes and are thus no longer taxable in the corporation's former country of residence.

Merger, Asset Transfer and Share Exchange

Assets may also leave a tax jurisdiction in cases of cross-border mergers. If, for example, G Corporation resident in country G is merged into F Corporation resident in country F, assets of G Corporation are transferred to F Corporation. After the legal merger is completed, country F has the right to tax the gains from the sale or use of the assets transferred. Country G has no tax claim from these gains because F Corporation is not subject to unlimited tax liability in country G. Again, if assets transferred belong to a permanent establishment in country G, country G still has a tax claim from the profits of the permanent establishment in terms of the limited tax liability of F Corporation.

Companies may also engage in asset transfers. When a domestic company transfers assets to a foreign corporation and in exchange receives shares in that corporation, the company's country of residence is no longer able to tax the hidden reserves of the assets transferred because it has to respect the foreign corporation as a distinct legal entity. In order to avoid a revenue loss, the country of residence can tax the gain upon the transfer of the assets. Again, if the assets transferred belong to a permanent establishment, the transferring company's residence country still has a tax claim on the hidden reserves transferred in terms of limited tax liability of the foreign corporation.

Shareholders may exchange shares in the course of business reorganization. When domestic shareholders exchange the shares in a domestic corporation against new shares in a foreign corporation (or vice versa) the share exchange may give raise to a capital gain and trigger income taxes. The shareholders` country of residence may refrain from immediately taxing the capital gain if subsequent gains from selling the new shares can be taxed.

Merger Directive

Within the European Union, the Merger Directive (MD) deals with cross-border business reorganizations. The MD is designed to avoid exit taxation of hidden reserves in cases where the tax claim of a Member State is not endangered. The MD covers legal mergers, legal divisions, outbound transfer of seat of European Corporations and of a Societas Europaea (S.E.), the transfer of assets and the exchange of shares. The MD stipulates that Member States shall refrain from taxing gains upon a cross-border restructuring subject to certain conditions. Companies involved in cross-border restructuring must be incorporated, resident in a Member State for tax purposes and subject to corporation tax. Tax exemption is only granted if the transferred assets can be attributed to a permanent establishment of the Member State of the transferring company. The latter requirement ensures the exit taxation of hidden reserves in cases where a Member State immediately forfeits its tax claim on the hidden reserves.

Example (1.7): German G Corporation transfers a German branch to British B Corporation. In turn British B Corporation issues shares to the transferring G Corporation. After the transfer of assets, B Corporation owns the assets belonging to the German branch. G Corporation holds shares in B Corporation. If the branch can be regarded as an independent business and as a permanent establishment of B Corporation in Germany, the transfer of assets belonging to the German permanent establishment is tax-exempt. B Corporation is subject to limited tax liability in Germany and, thus, Germany has the right to tax the profits of the permanent establishment.

In effect the MD grants the Member States the right to tax the hidden reserves related to assets which leave their jurisdiction on the occasion of a cross-border restructuring. As the MD upholds exit taxation, it does not enable companies to effectively engage in international tax rate arbitrage. On the other hand, the MD may not remove tax obstacles to cross-border restructuring in the European Market.

Reading List Chapter 1

Amatucci, Andrea: International Tax Law, Alphen aan den Rijn, 2006.

Ault, Huge J.; Arnold, Brian, J.: Comparative Income Taxation. A Structural Analysis, 3rd Edition. Alphen aan den Rijn, 2010.

Avery Jones, John F.: Avoiding Double Taxation: Credit versus Exemption - the Origins, in: Bulletin for International Taxation 2012, pp. 67-76.

Bittker, Boris I.; Eustice, James S.; Goldstein, Gersham: Federal Income Taxation of Corporation and Shareholders, 7th ed., Warren Gorham & Lamont, New York, 2000.

Endres, Dieter; Oestreicher, Andreas; Scheffler, Wolfram; Spengel, Christoph et al.: The Determination of Corporate Taxable Income in the EU Member States, Kluwer Law International, Alphen aan den Rijn, 2007.

Endres, Dieter; Spengel, Christoph; Brunsbach, Stefan; Miles, Andrew: Unternehmensbesteuerung in Deutschland, Corporate Taxation in Germany, 3rd ed., Düsseldorf, 2012.

Federal Ministry of Finance, Bundesministerium der Finanzen, Die wichtigsten Steuern im internationalen Vergleich, Berlin, 2012.

Finnerty, Chris; Merks, Paulus; Petriccione, Mario; Russo, Raffaele: Fundamentals of International Tax Planning, Amsterdam, 2007.

Haig, Robert M.: The Concept of Income: Economic and Legal Aspects, in: Haig, Robert M.: The Federal Income Tax, New York, 1921.

IBFD: Taxation of Companies in Europe, Amsterdam, 2009.

Jacobs, Otto H.; Endres, Dieter; Spengel, Christoph (eds.): Internationale Unternehmensbesteuerung, 7th ed., München, 2011.

Lang, Michael: Introduction to the Law of Double Taxation Conventions, Vienna, 2010.

Lang, Michael; Aigner, Hans-Jörgen; Scheuerle, Ulrich; Stefaner, Markus: CFC Legislation – Domestic Provisions, Tax Treaties and EC Law, Vienna, 2004.

Lodin, Sven-Olof; Gammie, Malcolm: Home State Taxation, Amsterdam, 2001.

Luckhaupt, Hagen; Overesch, Michael; Schreiber, Ulrich: The OECD Approach to Transfer Pricing. A Critical Assessment and Proposal, in: MPI Studies in Tax Law and Public Finance 1, Fundamentals of International Transfer Pricing in Law and Economics, Schön, Wolfgang; Konrad, Kai A. (eds.), München, 2012, S. 91-121.

Lüdicke, Jürgen: Exemption and Tax Credit in German Tax Treaties – Policy and Reality, in Bulletin for International Taxation 2010, pp. 609-619.

Miller, Angharad; Oats, Lynne: Principles of International Taxation, West Sussex, 2009.

OECD: International Tax Avoidance and Evasion – Four Related Studies, Paris, 1987.

OECD: Transfer Pricing Guidelines for Multinational Enterprises and Tax Administrations 2010, Paris, 2010.

OECD: Model Tax Convention on Income and Capital, Paris, 2010.

Oestreicher, Andreas; Spengel, Christoph: Tax Harmonization in Europe: The Determination of Corporate Taxable Income in the Member States, in: European Taxation 2007, pp. 437-451.

Spengel, Christoph; Oestreicher, Andreas; Koch, Reinald: How to Reform Taxation of Corporate Groups in Europe, in: World Tax Journal 2011, pp. 5-38.

Terra, Ben J.M.; Wattel, Peter J.: European Tax Law, 5th Edition, Alphen aan den Rijn, 2008.

van Boeijen-Ostaszewska, Ola; Schellekens, Marnix (eds.): European Tax Handbook 2012, Amsterdam, 2012.

Vermeend, Willem; Van der Ploeg, Rick; Timmer; Jan Willem: Taxes and the Economy 2008, Cheltenham.

Vogel, Klaus: Klaus Vogel on Double Taxation Conventions, 3rd ed., London, 1997.

2. Fundamentals of International Tax Planning

2.1. Cash Flow and Net Present Value

2.1.1. Equity Financed Investments

If investments have already been decided upon, ex-post tax planning may reduce the tax payments and may increase the investments' net cash flows. It is worth engaging in ex-post tax planning if the additional net cash flow exceeds the additional costs, e. g. costs of evaluating alternative tax designs, costs of tax consultancy and costs of legal advice. By contrast to ex-post tax planning, ex-ante tax planning may impact on investment and financing decisions, thereby increasing a company's after-tax cash flow. Cash flow is an important determinant of investment decisions. If external financing in terms of debt financing and equity financing is restricted, the cash flow generated by the company is the main source of finance (self-financing).

In the first place, international tax planning deals with tax rates which may vary across countries, with tax bases which may be affected by cross-border transactions because revenues are tax-exempt (e.g. foreign dividends) or because expenses may not be deducted (e.g. interest expenses). International tax planning also deals with the timing of tax payments. Under a proportional tax rate, future tax payments are preferred over tax payments which have to be settled immediately. Given a positive market interest rate, it is preferable to have cash available at an earlier point of time. Additional cash may increase financial investments and generate additional interest income.

Tax planning may increase an investor's private wealth, but it can also be favorable from a welfare perspective. If in an economy marginal investments are disadvantaged by taxes, taxation is responsible for underinvestment and thus for a welfare loss. Tax planning may have the potential to remove the obstacles to tax-disadvantaged investments. In this case, economic welfare is increased via tax planning.

Net Present Value

From a financial perspective, investors will invest if they think their wealth will increase. The profitability of real investments can be measured by the net present value (NPV). When calculating the NPV of a real investment, the real investment is compared to an alternative financial investment which yields the capital market interest rate. The NPV is subject to several assumptions. The most prominent assumption is the existence of a perfect and unrestricted capital market with a risk-free uniform interest rate for creditors and debtors. The market interest rate denotes the yield of the capital market investment, it indicates the market price for investing, lending or borrowing capital (cost of capital), and it denotes the price for deferring consumption as well as for bringing it forward.

Equity financed marginal investments generate the same return as the alternative financial investment in the capital market:

$$(2.1) \qquad C_0 = -I_0 + PV_0 = -I_0 + \textstyle\sum_{t=1}^{n} CF_t \cdot (1+i)^{-t} = 0.$$

The term CF_t denotes the cash flow (either cash inflow or cash outflow) at time t and the term i denotes the uniform, risk-free market interest rate. In case of a marginal investment, the initial investment outlay I_0 at time $t = 0$ equals the value of the discounted future cash flow PV_0 at time $t = 0$. A NPV of zero indicates that investors – in comparison to a capital market investment – do not obtain additional wealth by performing the equity financed real investment. The investments rate of return equals the market interest rate ($r = i$).

Profitable investments generate a higher return than the alternative capital market investment ($r > i$). The NPV of profitable investments is greater than zero ($PV_0 > I_0$). The investment increases the wealth of investors because the investors receive the value of discounted future cash flow PV_0 at time $t = 0$ which exceeds the invested amount of capital I_0 at time $t = 0$. The NPV denotes the additional wealth generated by the real investment which the investors can consume.

Net Present Value after Taxes

Taxes influence the NPV in two ways. First, taxes paid on profits reduce the investment's net cash flows. Taxes may also affect market prices, thus impacting on gross cash flows. The investors could, for example, shift the income tax burden to employees through lower wages or to customers through higher prices. In the following, it is assumed that the profit tax burden cannot be shifted away to other parties. All other things being equal, a reduction of the investment's net cash flows reduces the NPV.

Secondly, taxes affect the yield of the capital market investment. If the financial investment is taxed, the interest rate has to be cut by the tax rate applied to financial investments. This reduces the profitability of the capital market investment. The reduced market interest rate in isolation leads to an increase in the NPV after taxes. As a result, both the cash flow effect (enumerator) and the interest effect (denominator) of taxes impact on the after-tax NPV.

The NPV after taxes of an equity financed investment is calculated as:

$$(2.2) \qquad C_0^{\tau} = -I_0 + PV_0^{\tau} = -I_0 + \textstyle\sum_{t=1}^{n}(CF_t - T_t) \cdot (1+i_{\tau})^{-t}.$$

The net interest rate is defined as $i_\tau = i \cdot (1 - \tau_{FI})$ with the term τ_{FI} denoting the tax rate for financial investments. The tax liability T_t is determined as product of the tax rate and the tax base. Due to accrual accounting, the tax base of the income tax differs from the pre-tax cash flows. The most important deviation from the cash flow is caused by the depreciation of the investment outlay. If the investment outlay is classified as a depreciable asset, the acquisition or production costs are distributed over the useful life of the asset by means of scheduled depreciation for tax purposes. Therefore, the tax base is determined by deducting the tax depreciation D_t from the pre-tax cash flows. Given the proportional statutory tax rate τ_{RI}, which applies to profits, the profit tax payment at time t is determined as:

(2.3) $$T_t = \tau_{RI} \cdot (CF_t - D_t).$$

In case of a negative tax base (loss), Formula (2.3) implies an immediate tax refund.

Example (2.1): An individual investor invests 100 in an asset which has a useful life of two years. He or she faces an income tax rate of τ_{RI} = 45%. The profit tax base is calculated as pre-tax cash flow less the amount of depreciation of the asset (50 each year). The market interest rate amounts to 10%. The individual investor is subject to personal income tax on financial investments at a uniform rate of τ_{FI} = 25% and the net interest rate thus amounts to i_τ = 7.5%.

t	0	1	2
I_0	-100.00		
CF_t		60.00	55.00
D_t		50.00	50.00
CF_t - D_t		10.00	5.00
T_t		4.50	2.25
I_0 + CF_t - T_t	-100.00	55.50	52.75
NPV after taxes	$C_0^\tau = -100 + \frac{60 - 0.45 \cdot (60 - 50)}{1.075} + \frac{55 - 0.45 \cdot (55 - 50)}{1.075^2} = -2.73$		

In comparison to the investment's NPV before taxes which is zero (discounted at 10%), the value of discounted after-tax cash flows drops from PV_0 = 100 to PV_0^τ = 97.27 and the NPV after taxes drops from zero to -2.73. The real investment becomes unprofitable after taxes.

With respect to the tax effects on real investments, two effects can be discerned: the tax rate effect and the tax base effect. The tax rate effect depends on the relationship of the tax rates applying to real investment and to financial investment. Comparatively low real profit tax rates favor real investment ($\tau_{RI} < \tau_{FI}$). The tax base effect depends on the depreciation rules. Front-loaded depreciation advantages real investment because it reduces the tax base at the beginning of the investment period and defers the tax payments to the future. The resulting increase in net cash flow leads to additional interest income.

In the Example (2.1), the after-tax NPV is negative because of the tax rate differential between financial market investment and real investment. Both investments generate the same pre-tax return. The lower tax rate applicable to the financial investment favors the financial investment over the higher taxed real investment. Tax depreciation does not affect the NPV. If the NPV is calculated by applying a uniform tax rate of either 25% or 45%, the result is an after-tax NPV of zero. There is no timing effect. It is solely the tax rate differential (the tax rate effect) which matters.

If the tax base does not influence the after-tax profitability of the real investment and if the real investment's profit is taxed at the same rate as interest income generated by the financial investment ($\tau_{RI} = \tau_{FI} = \tau$), then the after-tax rate of return of the marginal investment, $r \cdot (1 - \tau)$, equals the after-tax rate of return of the financial investment, $i \cdot (1 - \tau)$. Under these conditions, the income tax has no effect on the marginal investment's NPV. The pre-tax NPV of the marginal investment ($C_0 = 0$) equals the after-tax NPV ($C_0^\tau = 0$).

Corporate Investment

If the investment is carried out by a corporation, the NPV calculation has to consider two levels of taxation. The corporation is subject to corporation tax and (if it is located in Germany) local trade tax at a combined tax rate of τ_C. The corporate tax burden amounts to

(2.4) $$TC_t = \tau_C \cdot (CF_t - D_t).$$

With respect to shareholder taxation, cash flow has to be classified as (taxable) dividend and (non-taxable) capital repayment. Dividends (DIV_t) are taxed at the individual dividend tax rate τ_D. If it is assumed that cash flow in the amount of depreciation is not distributed as a dividend, the dividend is defined as cash flow minus depreciation ($CF_t - D_t$) and dividend taxes amount to

(2.5) $$TD_t = \tau_D \cdot DIV_t = \tau_D \cdot (CF_t - D_t - TC_t).$$

The combined overall tax burden on corporation and shareholders amounts to:

(2.6) $$\begin{aligned} T_t = TC_t + TD_t &= [\tau_C + \tau_D * (1 - \tau_C)] \cdot (CF_t - D_t) \\ &= \tau_{RI} \cdot (CF_t - D_t) \end{aligned}$$

Regarding the financial investment, the individual shareholders are subject to individual income tax on the return of financial investments at a uniform tax rate τ_{FI}.

In the following, it is assumed that the equity capital is paid back in each period to the amount of the tax depreciation. Equity capital transferred to the shareholder is invested at the after-tax market rate of return. Thus, the net cash flow can be discounted at the market interest rate after individual income taxes.

Example (2.2): A German based corporation invests 100 equity capital in a depreciable asset (depreciation amounts to 50 per year). The combined corporation tax rate (corporation tax of 15% plus trade tax of 15%) amounts to $\tau_C = 30\%$. The market interest rate is 10%. Dividends and financial investments are taxed at a rate of $\tau_D = \tau_{FI} = 25\%$. The net interest rate amounts to $i_\tau = 7.5\%$.

t	0	1	2
I_0	-100.00		
CF_t		60.00	55.00
D_t		50.00	50.00
$CF_t - D_t$		10.00	5.00
TC_t		3.00	1.50
DIV_t		7.00	3.50
TD_t		1.75	0.88
$I_0 + CF_t - T_t$	-100.00	55.25	52.62
NPV after taxes	$C_0^\tau = -100 + \frac{60 - 0.475 \cdot (60-50)}{1.075} + \frac{55 - 0.475 \cdot (55-50)}{1.075^2} = -3.07$		

In comparison to the NPV before taxes, the value of after-tax discounted cash flows drops from $PV_0 = 100$ to $PV_0^\tau = 96.93$ and, as a result, the NPV drops from zero before taxes to -3.07 after taxes. The capital repayment, which equals the depreciation, (D_t) is tax-free. The investment becomes unprofitable after taxes due to the higher tax burden of the real investment compared to the financial investment.

The NPV of corporate investment, Example (2.2), is lower than the NPV of the natural person's investment, Example (2.1), indicating a tax disadvantage of the corporation. Distributed corporate profits are taxed twice, while profits earned by an individual are only taxed once. In the examples, the combined tax burden on the distributed corporate profits of 47.5% exceeds the individual income tax rate of 45%.

Given a tax disadvantage of distributed profits, the corporation experiences a tax incentive to defer profit distributions. A corporation's profit distribution policy depends on a comparison of the internal and the external rate of return. If the net return on capital within the corporation exceeds the net market interest rate available to the shareholders, profits should not be immediately distributed. Instead, profits should be retained and reinvested at the corporation's higher internal rate of return.

2.1.2. Debt Financed Investments

Investors have the choice of financing investments with equity capital or with debt. In the case of debt financing, the investment's NPV has to reflect the cash flow connected with the loan. Given a perfect capital market with a uniform risk-free market interest rate, the pre-tax NPV of a loan is zero because the interest rate on the loan equals the market interest rate. Under these assumptions, debt financing of an investment does not change the investment´s pre-tax NPV.

Taxes may change this result. Interest payments are tax-deductible and reduce profit taxes, which increases an investment's after tax NPV. From this perspective, debt financing generates a tax shield for the investor. On the other hand, interest income is subject to tax. Taking into account both tax effects, debt financing may impact on the after-tax NPV of a debt financed investment.

The NPV after taxes of a debt financed investment with L_t as the amount of debt at time t and R_t as the repayment of debt at time t amounts to

$$\begin{aligned} C_0^\tau &= -I_0 + PV_0^\tau + PVL_0^\tau \\ PVL_0^\tau &= L_0 - \textstyle\sum_{t=1}^{n}[(1-\tau_{RI})\cdot r\cdot L_{t-1} + R_t]\cdot(1+i_\tau)^{-t} \\ R_t &= L_{t-1} - L_t \\ L_0 &= \textstyle\sum_{t=1}^{n} R_t \end{aligned} \tag{2.7}$$

Taxes influence the after-tax NPV of debt capital (PVL_0^τ) through the tax deductibility of interest payments ($r \cdot L_{t-1}$) and through the after-tax discount factor. Given a uniform tax rate ($\tau_{RI} = \tau_{FI}$) and a uniform interest rate ($r = i$), the after-tax NPV of debt capital amounts to zero. In this case, granting a loan is not preferred over a capital market investment. The advantage of tax-deductible interest payments equals the disadvantage of taxable interest income. Once the assumption of a uniform tax rate is dropped, taxes interfere with financing decisions because tax savings and tax payments no longer correspond to each other.

Example (2.3): In the above Example (2.1), the individual investor faces an income tax rate of τ_{RI} = 45%. The market interest rate amounts to 10%. The investor finances the investment with debt at an interest rate of 10%. Interest income is taxed at a uniform rate of τ_{FI} = 25% and the loan's net interest rate thus equals the net market interest rate i_τ = 7.5%.

t	0	1	2
L_0	100.00		
$r \cdot L_{t-1}$		10.00	5.00
R_t		50.00	50.00
$\tau_{RI} \cdot r \cdot L_{t-1}$		4.50	2.25
L_0-R_t - $r \cdot L_{t-1} \cdot (1 - \tau_{RI})$	100.00	55.50	52.75
NPV after taxes	$PVL_0^\tau = 100 - \frac{50 + 10 \cdot (1 - 45\%)}{1.075} - \frac{50 + 5 \cdot (1 - 45\%)}{1.075^2} = +2.73$		

The NPV of the loan amounts to 2.73. The positive NPV reflects the tax advantage of debt financing caused by the tax rate differential of 20 percentage points.

Given the NPV C_0^τ = -2.73 of the real investment in Example (2.1), the overall NPV of a debt financed investment according to equation (2.7) is thus zero, C_0^τ = -100 + 97.27 +2.73 = 0. By debt financing the investor avoids the tax disadvantage of a profit tax rate τ_{RI}, which is higher than the tax rate τ_{FI} on interest income.

Shareholder Debt Financing

In the presence of tax rate differentials concerning equity financing and debt financing, the shareholders of corporations may switch from equity to debt. Debt financing is preferred over equity financing if the combined tax rate on dividend income is higher than the combined tax rate on interest income. If interest income does not trigger taxes on the level of the corporation, shareholders compare the combined tax rate on distributed profits $\tau_{RI} = \tau_C + \tau_D - \tau_C \cdot \tau_D$ with the tax rate on interest income τ_{FI}.

Example (2.4): In the above Example (2.2) of the corporate investment, the combined corporation tax rate amounts to $\tau_C = 30\%$. The corporation finances the investment with a loan. Interest payments are fully tax-deductible for the corporation (the partial non-deductibility for trade tax purposes in case of a German corporation is ignored). The market interest rate equals the loan´s interest rate and amounts to 10%. Dividends and interest income are taxed at a rate of $\tau_D = \tau_{FI} = 25\%$. The combined dividend tax rate is $\tau_{RI} = 47.50\% = 30\% + 25\% - 30\% \cdot 25\%$. The net interest rate amounts to $i_\tau = 7.5\%$.

t	0	1	2
L_0	100.00		
$r \cdot L_{t-1}$		10.00	5.00
R_t		50.00	50.00
$\tau_{RI} \cdot r \cdot L_{t-1}$		4.75	2.38
$L_0 - R_t - r \cdot L_{t-1} \cdot (1 - \tau_{RI})$	100.00	55.25	52.643
NPV after taxes	$PVL_0^\tau = 100 - \frac{50+10\cdot(1-47{,}50\%)}{1.075} - \frac{50+5\cdot(1-47{,}50\%)}{1.075^2} = 3.07$		

The after-tax NPV of the loan amounts to $PVL_0^\tau = 3.07$ reflecting the tax advantage of debt financing the corporate investment. Given the after-tax NPV of $C_0^\tau = -3.07$ of the real corporate investment in Example (2.2), the overall after-tax NPV of the debt financed investment according to equation (2.7) amounts to zero ($C_0^\tau = -100 + 96.93 + 3.07 = 0$). Debt financing substitutes an overall tax burden on distributed profits of 47.50% with a tax burden of 25% on interest income. The total after-tax NPV effect of debt financing is caused by the tax rate differential of 22.50% (= 47.50% – 25%) related to the corporate profit before interest payments ($3.07 = 22.50\% \cdot 10 \cdot 1.075^{-1} + 22.50\% \cdot 5 \cdot 1.075^{-2}$).

The management of closely held corporations has information concerning the tax situation of the shareholders and is able to calculate the after-tax NPV by taking into account the shareholders' individual taxation with respect to dividends and interest income. Conversely, if the corporation's management has no reliable information on the tax situation of the shareholders, only the corporation tax burden can be taken into account. Particularly the management of publicly held companies with many shareholders from different tax jurisdictions must ignore shareholder taxation and discount cash flows after corporation taxes at the gross market interest rate.

Companies accessing the global capital market face the world capital market rate of return which is not influenced by personal income taxation. Capital market investors who are differently taxed at the personal level end up with different after tax returns. To put it differently, in a global capital market, a corporate investor's benchmark of profitability is the gross market interest rate.

2.2. Investment Shifting and Profit Shifting

International tax planning aims at taking advantage of tax rate as well as tax base differentials across countries. A multinational company operating under tax laws granting a single country the exclusive right to tax profits, has an incentive to invest in low-tax countries. By shifting real investments to countries where profit taxes are low, a multinational company may increase the company's after-tax cash flow and market value. The same is true if multinational companies are engaged in international acquisitions. By acquiring low-taxed companies, the multinational company's profit tax burden decreases and its market value increases.

International tax planning is not restricted to real investment shifting and cross-border acquisitions. Multinational companies may also shift tax bases from high-tax countries to low-tax countries without shifting investments. Profits can be shifted by internal transactions. A subsidiary, for example, located in a low-tax country delivering goods to an affiliated subsidiary located in high-tax country may charge a high transfer price for the goods delivered. The profit of the delivering subsidiary increases, whereas the profit of the receiving subsidiary decreases. As a result, profit is shifted from a high-taxed subsidiary to a low-taxed subsidiary. The multinational company takes advantage of international tax rate differentials.

The same tax effect can be achieved by debt financing of subsidiaries located in high-tax countries by corporations located in low-tax countries. Interest payments, as a rule, are tax-deductible and create a tax shield in the high-tax country. Interest payments received are subject to tax in the low-tax country. Again, profit is shifted from the high-tax country to the low-tax country and the multinational can take advantage of the international tax rate differential.

European Tax Planning

Europe is an especially challenging area for international tax planning because there are remarkable differences in corporation tax rates across European countries. European countries, as other countries all over the world, compete for both real investments and income tax bases by lowering their corporation tax rate.[10] Internationally diverging corporation tax rates give rise to international tax planning by means of tax rate arbitrage. The creation of a single market within the European Union and the accession of Member States from Central and Eastern Europe to the European Union have intensified tax competition in Europe.

---

[10] In the EU, in recent years, a decline in statutory corporation tax rates has taken place, which may be termed "race to the bottom". Nevertheless, there is still a considerable corporate tax burden and the Member States do not suffer from a substantial loss of corporation tax revenue. Member States still seem to be able to tax profits connected to a certain location (local rents) or stemming from public goods, such as the country´s legal system and infrastructure. Member States have successfully broadened the tax base to compensate for the declining tax rates. Triggered by comparatively low tax rates, more companies seem to have chosen the legal form of a corporation.

European Directives address taxes charged on cross-border dividends, interest and royalty payments, and are aimed at the enhancement of the internal market. These directives remove tax impediments on cross-border flows of investment income.

Parent Subsidiary Directive and Interest and Royalties Directive

The purpose of the Parent Subsidiary Directive (PSD) is the elimination of double taxation on inter-corporate dividends. The PSD stipulates that (i) the country of residence of the subsidiary may not levy a withholding tax on intra-EU dividends (Art. 5 PSD) and that (ii) the country of residence of the parent has to apply either the exemption method or the credit method (ordinary credit) for incoming dividends (Art. 4 PSD). The deduction of management costs and interest payments related to the shareholding can be disallowed in the country of the parent, if the amount does not exceed 5% of the dividend. The entities have to qualify as resident incorporated companies of a Member State subject to corporation tax. The parent must hold at least 10% of the equity capital of the subsidiary. Member States may require an uninterrupted holding period of a maximum of 2 years.

The Interest and Royalties Directive (IRD) aims at avoiding double taxation which may arise because the source country levies a withholding tax on the gross income, while the country of residence taxes the net profit (i.e. net of all costs incurred). The IRD stipulates that the source country may not levy a withholding tax on any inter-corporate interest payments or royalty payments including payments from or to permanent establishments (Art. 1 Para. 1 IRD). Interest is defined as income from debt claims of any kind, whether or not carrying a right to participate in the debtor's profits. Royalties are defined as payments from the use of intangible assets, such as copyrights, patents, trade-marks, and know-how. The entity must be incorporated in a Member State, has to be resident in a Member State for tax purposes and has to be subject to corporation tax. A company must hold at least 25% of the equity capital of another company, or a third company must hold at least 25% of the capital of both companies. Member States can require an uninterrupted holding period of up to 2 years.

PSD and IRD facilitate international tax planning because both directives eliminate withholding taxes in the source country. Moreover, the PSD ensures that profits earned by a subsidiary are only taxed once. Because Member States usually exempt foreign dividends from the corporation tax base, the dividends are only burdened with the foreign corporation tax on the profit, enabling parent companies to take advantage of low foreign corporation taxes.

European Treaty

EU companies engaging in international tax planning may make use of the single market which is characterized by tax law divergence. The European Court of Justice (ECJ) has constantly stated that it is not unlawful to take advantage of low-tax rates in another Member State. By granting fundamental economic freedoms, the Treaty on the Functioning of the European Union (TFEU) makes it difficult for

Member States to fight tax planning of multinational companies aimed at exploiting tax rate differentials. Member States have to adjust their tax legislation to the European Treaty. Member States are neither allowed to discriminate against foreign investors or foreign investments nor to disadvantage foreign investments of domestic investors.

Tax Harmonization

Given the influence of taxes on economic activities in the single market, harmonization of the corporation tax base and the corporation tax rates has become a political issue. Harmonized European corporation tax rules might effectively combat international tax planning and improve the functioning of the single market. Common rules to determine the taxable profit of European companies seems to have the potential to overcome one of the most challenging problems of international company taxation: the allocation of the tax base between countries. A Common Consolidated Corporate Tax Base (CCCTB) as is proposed by the European commission[11] eliminates the complexities of transfer pricing within Europe and copes with the high costs of complying with the corporation tax system.

2.3. International Tax Planning and Residence-Based Taxation

In point of fact, tax harmonization is not necessary to combat international tax planning and international double taxation. Instead, the taxing right can be assigned to the residence state of the investor. Under the pure residence principle combined with the worldwide income principle, the country where legal or natural persons have their tax residence has the exclusive right to tax worldwide income of those persons. Consequently, double taxation of foreign income is avoided.

Worldwide income consists of both foreign and domestic earnings. The residence principle implies that foreign and domestic earnings are equally treated from the residence country's point of view. Foreign losses are part of the worldwide income, i.e. losses can be fully claimed in the residence country of the investors. Immediate compensation of foreign losses and subsequent taxation of foreign profits are inherent in a residence-based tax system. Immediate loss compensation is also achieved if taxpayers suffer from domestic losses and earn foreign profits.

Capital Export Neutrality

The pure residence principle restricts tax planning activities by ensuring capital export neutrality of income taxation (CEX). Because all income from capital is taxed in the investors' state of residence, the profitability of investments does not depend on the place of the investment. Given equal gross yields, the net yield of

[11] European Commission (2011).

the foreign investment equals the net yield of a comparable domestic investment, irrespective of the foreign tax level.

Different tax rates across residence countries influence the after-tax rates of return, but the pre-tax rates of return remain unaffected by taxation. Given a domestic and a foreign marginal investment with the pre-tax rates of return r_D and r_F respectively, investor H resident of country H facing the income tax rate τ_H and investor L resident of country L facing the income tax rate τ_L, with $\tau_H \neq \tau_L$, determine the investments' after-tax rate of return by taking into account the respective domestic tax rate. Investor H determines the after-tax rate of return $r_F \cdot (1 - \tau_H) = r_D \cdot (1 - \tau_H)$, whereas investor L determines the after-tax rate of return $r_F \cdot (1 - \tau_L) = r_D \cdot (1 - \tau_L)$. Irrespective of the different tax rates, that both investors face, the investment decisions remain unaffected by taxes. If the capital market investment is also taxed at the tax rates τ_H and τ_L respectively, the marginal investment is not affected by taxes, because $r_F \cdot (1 - \tau_H) = i \cdot (1 - \tau_H)$ and $r_F \cdot (1 - \tau_L) = i \cdot (1 - \tau_L)$.

If all countries apply the pure residence principle and uniformly tax all types of capital income, a uniform (worldwide) interest rate results and the capital is internationally allocated according to the investments' gross yields. International production efficiency prevails, i.e. the marginal productivity of capital is equalized worldwide and the total amount of (worldwide) capital is efficiently allocated.

Low taxes generate a tax incentive for investors to transfer their tax residence from high-tax countries to low-tax countries. Upon the transfer of residence, the income taxes on worldwide income are reduced and the amount of net-income available for consumption increases. Yet, investment location decisions are not altered by the investor's transfer of residence, if the transfer of residence itself does not trigger taxes in the former country of residence. The pure residence principle precludes any incentive to shift profits or real investments across countries. Income taxes do not distort the decision where to locate the investment. Countries do not have an incentive to lower the tax rate in order to attract foreign investments. Worldwide taxation is production efficient and conforms to CEX.

Ownership Neutrality

The bidder for the ownership rights of a company may be able to increase the company's value after the acquisition because the company's costs are reduced or the company's revenues are increased due to synergy effects. As a result, the bidder's maximum offer price may be higher than the company's value for the present owner (the present owner's minimum price). If the bidder's maximum price exceeds the owners minimum price, the transfer of the ownership rights is in the interest of both parties. The ownership rights of the firm (e.g. the shares of a corporation) are transferred to the more efficient owner. Taxes should not prevent such an economically advantageous transfer of ownership rights just as they should not encourage such a transfer in the absence of economic advantages (ownership neutrality).

A pure residence-based income tax system ensures ownership neutrality, if pre-tax and post-tax prices of a company's seller and buyer do not differ. Consider the simple case of a perpetual annuity. The target company generates a perpetual profit (cash flow) *PR* and the market interest rate amounts to *i*. The pre-tax value of the target company is

(2.8) $$V = \frac{PR}{i}.$$

The seller and the buyer are taxed on profits and on interest income at the uniform rates τ_S and τ_B respectively ($\tau_S \neq \tau_B$). The after-tax value of the company amounts to

(2.9) $$V^{\tau} = \frac{PR \cdot (1-\tau_S)}{i \cdot (1-\tau_S)} = \frac{PR \cdot (1-\tau_B)}{i \cdot (1-\tau_B)} = \frac{PR}{i}.$$

Although the tax rates are different, the seller and the buyer determine the same value of the company. The respective countries of residence generate tax revenue without altering the value of the target company if profits and interest income are taxed at the same tax rate. Cash flow effect (enumerator) and interest effect (denominator) of taxation cancel out. With pure residence-based taxation, ownership neutrality is preserved if the countries' income tax systems are neutral with respect to investment decisions.

If investments are not neutrally taxed, residence-based taxation has the potential to distort the allocation of ownership rights. Because the impact of taxes on the value of investments depends on the investor's tax residence, low-taxed investors may be tax-advantaged compared with high-taxed investors when competing for a company's ownership rights.

Example (2.5): Investor L resident in the low-tax country L and investor H, resident in the high-taxed country H, both bid for the ownership rights of S Company, located in country S. The price of S Company depends on the profit taxes to be paid by the bidder. If both investors discount the company's cash flows at the same discount rate, investor L enjoys a tax advantage in the bidding process.

Because a residence-based income tax system does not necessarily ensure ownership neutrality, it may result in competitive disadvantages of resident multinational companies.

Corporation Tax

The pure residence principle does not respect the fact that corporations as legally distinct entities shield their profits from the shareholders' income tax. Thus, real world tax systems, accepting the corporation as a legally distinct taxpayer, do not conform to pure residence-based tax systems. Under the pure residence principle, foreign retained corporate profits are to be included in the worldwide income of the domestic shareholders. The same is true for foreign corporate losses. Worldwide corporate profits and corporate losses are pooled at the shareholder level.

2.4. International Tax Planning and Source-Based Taxation

With the pure source principle, the income generated by an economic activity located in the source country is exclusively taxed in that country. The investor's country of residence does not tax the foreign income. Double taxation of foreign income is averted. The source principle implies a ban on tax deduction for all payments on capital in the source country, such as interest payments, license fees and royalty payments. Correspondingly, the country of residence does not tax the foreign investment income. Foreign losses reduce the income derived in the source country. In the residence country, foreign losses are disregarded.

Capital Import Neutrality

Because all capital income is taxed in the source country, the source principle ensures capital import neutrality (CIN). CIN prevails if the overall tax burden of an investment is exclusively determined by a source country's income taxes. Differences in tax rates across source countries result in different after-tax rates of return.

Given a marginal investment in source country H with the pre-tax rate of return r and the market interest rate i which are both taxed at the income tax rate τ_H, all investors determine the investments' after-tax rate of return $r \cdot (1 - \tau_H) = i \cdot (1 - \tau_H)$. A marginal investment in source country L, which is taxed at the income tax rate τ_L, yields the after-tax rate of return $r \cdot (1 - \tau_L) = i \cdot (1 - \tau_L)$. If the tax rates in both countries are the same, income taxes do not distort the capital allocation because the investments' after-tax rate of return is the same in both countries. If the tax rates differ ($\tau_H \neq \tau_L$), the investment's after-tax rate of return depends on the investment's location.

Differences in the countries' tax rates are reflected in the investments' pre-tax rates of return. Investors are indifferent between investing in country H at the pre-tax return r_H and investing in country L at the pre-tax return r_L if the after-tax returns in both countries are the same: $r_H \cdot (1 - \tau_H) = r_L \cdot (1 - \tau_L) = i_H \cdot (1 - \tau_H) = i_L \cdot (1 - \tau_L)$. Given different tax rates across countries, this indifference condition implies diverging pre-tax rates of return ($r_H \neq r_L$ and $i_H \neq i_L$). Investors engage in tax rate arbitrage, increase investments in the low-tax country driving down the investments' pre-tax rate of return in the low-tax country. International tax rate arbitrage brings about a uniform (worldwide) net interest rate.

Example (2.6): Assume a pre-tax rate of return of 10% and income tax rates of 25% and 50% in countries A and B respectively. The after-tax rates of return are 7.5% in country A and 5% in country B. Investors increase investment in country A. The capital inflow to country A reduces the pre-tax rate of return investors can earn in country A. Once the pre-tax rate of return in country A is reduced to 6.67%, the after-tax rate of return amounts to 5% (= 6.67 – 25% · 6.67). The after-tax rates of return are the same in both countries.

The marginal productivity of capital invested in a country with a higher tax rate must be higher than in a country with a lower tax rate. As a result, investment decisions depend on the countries' tax rates. Because after-tax returns are equalized across countries whereas pre-tax returns of marginal investments may differ across countries, capital is inefficiently allocated. Thus, CIN is production-inefficient. Countries may attract additional investments by lowering their tax rates.

Ownership Neutrality

Source-based taxation does not distort the allocation of ownership rights. The buyer's and the seller's tax position in their respective residence countries is irrelevant. The tax burden depends solely on the location of the target company, and all bidders for the ownership rights of the target company face the same tax burden.

Example (2.7): Investor L resident in the low-tax country L and investor H, resident in the high-taxed country H, bid for the ownership rights of S Company, located in country S. The price of S Company only depends on the taxes paid by S Company. As investor L pays the same taxes than investor H, the bidding process is not distorted by taxes.

A uniform tax rate τ on profits and interest income generated in the source country ensures ownership neutrality. Assume again a target company generating a perpetual profit (cash flow) PR and a market interest rate i. The after-tax value of the company

(2.10) $$V^{\tau} = \frac{PR \cdot (1-\tau)}{i \cdot (1-\tau)} = \frac{PR}{i}$$

equals the company's pre-tax value. To ensure ownership neutrality, the tax system of the source country must not necessarily operate with a single tax rate. If profit is taxed at rate τ_P and interest income is taxed at τ_I ($\tau_P \neq \tau_I$) the company's after tax value

(2.11) $$V^{\tau} = \frac{PR \cdot (1-\tau_P)}{i \cdot (1-\tau_I)} \neq \frac{PR}{i}$$

is not identical with the company's pre-tax value V. However, ownership neutrality is still preserved because the buyer and the seller face the same taxes in the source country. Taxes impact on the company's value, but do not distort the transfer of ownership rights. The ownership rights of the company are transferred to the more efficient owner.

Level Playing Field

The source principle may be justified on the grounds of leveling the playing field for investors in the source country. Foreign investors face the same taxes as domestic investors. Thus, all investments in the source country are equally taxed. Because all companies located in the source country face the same taxes, source-based taxation does not distort competition in the source country.

Yet, companies competing on the world market do not necessarily face the same tax burden. If, for example, a U.S. based company produces in the U.S. and sells its products in France, a market where the U.S. company competes with a French company producing and selling the same products, the tax burden of the two companies is determined by U.S. and French taxes respectively and thus may be different although both companies are competitors in the same country.

Tax Compliance and Tax Administration

Source-based taxation may have advantages in terms of compliance and administrative costs. Investors face exclusively the tax authority of the source country. The source countries tax administration can rely on local information and need not gather information on worldwide capital income. Moreover, source-based taxation is compatible with the taxation of legally distinct entities, e.g. corporations. Corporations resident in the source country can be taxed according to current tax rules and in accordance with the source principle.

Nevertheless, a pure source-based system cannot be found in any country of the world. Interest expenses, royalties and the like are, as a rule, tax-deductible in the source country.

2.5. International Tax Planning under Hybrid Tax Systems

Real world tax systems conform neither to the pure source principle, nor to the pure residence principle. All countries have implemented elements of both taxation regimes, thus forming hybrid tax systems. A hybrid tax system provides investors with an implicit option as to where to be taxed and consequently generates tax planning opportunities.

Inconsistencies of Residence-Based Taxation

Some countries, most prominently the U.S., rely on the residence principle and tax their residents' worldwide income. Taxes paid in foreign countries are credited against domestic taxes on foreign income (foreign tax credit). The domestic income tax rate τ_H is reduced by the foreign income tax rate τ_F. After the foreign tax credit, the applicable tax rate for foreign investments (τ_{RI}) equals the domestic tax rate

(2.12) $$\tau_{RI} = (\tau_H - \tau_F) + \tau_F = \tau_H$$

Investors do not have an incentive to shift real investments to low tax countries. The tax burden does not depend on the investment's location.

Example (2.8): Investor I is resident of country R. R has implemented residence based income taxation. I considers an equity financed real investment in country S through a permanent establishment. The investment outlay amounts to 100 and is invested in an asset with a useful life of two years. In country S, the investor is taxed at a rate of τ_F = 20% (limited tax liability). In country R, I is taxed at a rate of τ_H = 45% (unlimited tax liability). The tax bases in both countries are the same (pre-tax cash flow minus depreciation). Interest income is taxed by country R at a rate of τ_{FI}= 25%.

t	0	1	2
I_0	-100.00		
CF_t		60.00	55.00
$CF_t - D_t$		10.00	5.00
$\tau_F \cdot (CF_t - D_t)$		2.00	1.00
$(\tau_H - \tau_F) \cdot (CF_t - D_t)$		4.50	2.25
$I_0 + CF_t - T_t$	-100.00	55.50	52.75
NPV after taxes	$C_0^\tau = -100 + \frac{55.50}{1.075} + \frac{52.75}{1.075^2} = -2.73$		

The investment's tax burden is determined by the residence country's tax rate τ_H = 45%. The investor cannot take advantage of the low income tax rate in country S. As the discount rate is determined by the tax rate of the country of residence as well, the investment's tax burden does not depend on its location. Therefore, the foreign investment's NPV of C_0^τ = -2.73 is identical with the NPV of a comparable equity financed domestic investment (see Example (2.1)).

The foreign tax credit is limited (ordinary tax credit). Credit is not granted beyond the domestic tax level if foreign taxes are higher (excess credit). In this case ($\tau_F > \tau_H$), the ordinary tax credit effectively works like the exemption method, i.e. domestic taxes are not levied on foreign income. Thus, in an excess credit situation, the investment's net return is determined by the foreign tax rate ($\tau_{RI} = \tau_F$). High foreign tax rates deter cross-border investments. Tax planning aims at mixing foreign income in order to overcome restrictions on the tax credit.

Income from a high-tax country may be pooled with income from a low-tax country to avoid domestic taxation of foreign income altogether. Special tax rules are targeted against this type of tax planning.

Real world residence-based tax systems respect corporations as legally distinct entities. Current inclusion of foreign corporate profits and losses in the worldwide income of the domestic shareholders, as demanded by the pure residence principle, is not feasible for legal as well as for administrative reasons. From a legal perspective, the foreign corporation is a resident of the foreign country. The shareholders´ country of residence does not have the right to tax the income of the foreign corporation. From an administrative perspective, it may be very difficult to gather the relevant information about the income of foreign corporations. Information concerning the profits of closely held foreign corporations may be available to domestic shareholders. Minority shareholders of publicly owned corporations, however, have no access to the information necessary to determine the taxable income of the foreign corporation.

Given the legal and tax data restrictions, current inclusion of foreign subsidiaries' profits is very seldom in practice. Denmark and Italy are the only EU countries which employ an optional residence-based corporate taxation scheme. Both countries apply current inclusion only to corporate groups and stop at the level of the corporate parent. The foreign profits included in the parent's tax computation are not passed onto the parent's own shareholders.

Nevertheless, many countries have implemented current inclusion regimes targeted at low-taxed foreign corporations used by domestic shareholders to shelter capital income from domestic taxation. In such cases, a foreign corporation's retained profit may be taxed as ordinary income of the domestic shareholders.

Where current inclusion rules do not apply, domestic income taxation of a foreign corporation's retained profits is deferred. As long as the foreign corporate profits are retained, domestic income taxes are not levied on those profits. The foreign corporation´s profits are only burdened with foreign corporation taxes.[12] Upon distribution to a domestic corporation, profits are subject to domestic corporation taxes and foreign corporation taxes are credited. The longer the distribution of profits is deferred, the lower is the NPV of shareholder income taxes and the more pronounced is the effect of foreign taxes on the net return. As a consequence, the profit distribution policy of foreign corporations influences the overall tax burden of foreign corporate profits which is not compatible with pure residence-based income taxation.

Inconsistencies of Source-Based Taxation

Most continental European countries apply the residence principle and tax worldwide income. Yet, the double taxation treaties these countries have concluded make use of the exemption method. The right to tax profits attributed to foreign

---

[12] If the domestic shareholder (the parent company) is in need of cash, the foreign corporation could grant a loan to the shareholder, thereby avoiding the taxable distribution of foreign profits.

permanent establishments is regularly waived by the investors' country of residence. Because corporations are respected as legally distinct entities as well, the respective countries do not tax retained profits of foreign corporations either. Insofar, the source principle applies. By contrast, the residence principle applies to royalties, license fees and interest income derived in foreign countries. These payments are tax-deductible abroad and subject to tax in the country of residence of the recipient. As a consequence, the international tax regimes of these countries exempt foreign profits, whilst taxing other foreign capital income.

A hybrid tax system exempting foreign profits from domestic taxation, but burdening income from capital market investment with domestic taxes may create a strong incentive to shift real investment to low-tax countries.

Example (2.9): The natural person I is a resident of country R. R exempts foreign profits from domestic taxes. I considers an equity financed real investment in country S via a permanent establishment. In source country S, the investor is taxed at a rate of $\tau_F = 20\%$ (limited tax liability). The tax base is determined as pre-tax cash flow minus depreciation. Interest income from capital market investments is taxed by residence country R at a rate of $\tau_{FI} = 25\%$.

t	0	1	2
I_0	-100.00		
CF_t		60.00	55.00
D_t		50.00	50.00
$CF_t - D_t$	0	10.00	5.00
$\tau_F \cdot (CF_t - D_t)$	0	2.00	1.00
$I_0 + CF_t - T_t$	-100.00	58.00	54.00
NPV after taxes	$C_0^\tau = -100 + \frac{60 - 0.2 \cdot (60 - 50)}{1.075} + \frac{55 - 0.2 \cdot (55 - 50)}{1.075} = +0.68$		

The investor takes advantage of the lower income tax rate in country S. Because the investment is burdened with income tax of $\tau_F = 20\%$, whereas the alternative capital market investment triggers taxes at a rate of $\tau_{FI} = 25\%$, the NPV rises to $C_0^\tau = 0.68$. Compared to domestic case (see Example (2.1)), the investment becomes profitable after taxes.

The application of the exemption method to foreign profits is in line with the source principle. Yet, the market return on capital of the financial investment is burdened with residence-based taxes which conflicts with the source principle. From a tax perspective, the benchmark for investments worldwide is determined by residence-based taxes, while the real investment's tax burden depends on the place of investment. Obviously, such a hybrid tax system may distort real investment decisions.

Financing decision may be distorted by taxes as well. As capital income is not uniformly taxed, investors are able to engage in international tax rate arbitrage. Corporate investments in low-tax countries are financed with equity, while corporate investments in high-tax countries are financed with debt. Equity financing of a foreign corporation's investments results in foreign profits subject to foreign corporation taxes. Deferring the distribution of low-taxed foreign corporate profits increases the profitability of equity financed foreign investments. Conversely, debt financing results in tax-deductible interest payments in the foreign country thereby avoiding foreign taxes. Interest income is taxed in the residence country of the creditor.

Residence Based versus Source Based Taxation

Companies resident in countries which predominantly rely on the residence principle, as the U.S., may experience a competitive disadvantage compared to companies resident in countries which rely on the source principle. Given the pre-tax return of the investment in the source country, the net return depends on the tax system of the investors' state of residence. The investors resident in a country with source-based profit taxation take advantage of low taxes in the source country. Conversely, the investors resident in a country with residence-based profit taxation may face the higher income taxes of their home country.

With respect to corporate investment, in principle the same is true. Under residence-based taxation, foreign dividends are taxed, while under source-based taxation foreign dividends are exempt. This is especially important when ownership rights of corporations are transferred. All other things being equal, bidders resident in a country which exempts foreign dividends offer a higher price than bidders who have to take into account additional domestic taxes on foreign dividends. Consequently, shareholders resident in countries with source based dividend taxation may specialize in low-taxed foreign corporations. Yet, irrespective of the tax system in the shareholders′ country of residence, taxes on dividends can be deferred, thus leveling the playing field in a bidding process for shareholders resident in countries with different dividend taxation schemes.

2.6. Legal Restrictions on Tax Planning

2.6.1. General Anti-Abuse Rules

The need for anti-abuse rules seems to be less pronounced in countries relying on residence-based taxation compared to countries relying on source-based taxation. However, not a single country in the world has implemented the pure residence principle which is resistant against international investment shifting and profit shifting. Anti-abuse rules targeted at international tax planning exist virtually in all countries, whatever mechanism of avoiding double taxation (exemption method vs. credit method) the countries may employ.

Because the corporations are internationally accepted as legally distinct entities, irrespective of the implementation of either the source principle or the residence principle, countries with worldwide taxation and a foreign tax credit, as the U.S., basically employ the same anti-abuse rules as countries which exempt foreign profits, as Spain, France and Germany. High-tax countries particularly need anti-avoidance rules targeted at excessive debt financing and tax deferral in low-taxed companies.

Tax Planning versus Tax Fraud

Tax planning (or tax avoidance) is characterized by making use of the legal rules in order to reduce tax payments. Tax planning opportunities are sometimes explicitly offered by the tax law itself, e.g. accelerated depreciation instead of straight-line depreciation. In many cases the legal rules offer implicit options, e.g. the choice between a foreign permanent establishment or a foreign subsidiary and the choice between financing with equity or with debt.

Tax planning is respected by the tax law as long as the taxpayers assert economic reasons for choosing a specific location or a specific legal form for his investment. The courts rule in favor of the taxpayers if their decisions are not taken for the sole purpose of avoiding taxes. Consequently, taxpayers may arrange their business affairs to keep taxes low as long as they comply with the law.

Taxpayers commit tax fraud if an action contravenes the law (e.g., taxpayers do not disclose all relevant information, disclose wrong information or falsify documents or accounts). Tax fraud is prosecuted under criminal law.

Restrictions on Tax Planning

The tax law restricts tax planning opportunities if specific types of tax planning are considered to be harmful to the national tax revenue. Countries make use of general anti-abuse rules. General anti-abuse rules deny tax advantages if they have been achieved by implementing a tax planning strategy which is inappropriate in both legal and economic terms and serves the sole or main purpose of saving taxes (*fraus legis*). Such general anti-abuse rules may not be applicable, if the taxpayers can give significant non-tax reasons for having chosen this strategy. As a rule, business decisions concerning the location or the legal form of investments are not within the scope of general anti-abuse rules. It is usually possible for the taxpayers to present non-tax evidence for the choice of a certain legal form or of a certain location.

Regarding investment within the European Union, the European Court of Justice has clarified that general anti-abuse rules are not appropriate to combat international tax planning which may be considered harmful by Member States.[13] Therefore, Member States have implemented a wide range of specific anti-abuse

---

[13] See Leur-Blom (C-28/95).

rules in order to qualify certain tax planning strategies as undue tax avoidance, even if such tax planning does not constitute *fraus legis* in the sense of general anti-abuse rules. In the following, two common specific anti-abuse rules are briefly described.

2.6.2. Specific Anti-Abuse Rules

2.6.2.1. Controlled Foreign Corporations Legislation

Controlled Foreign Corporations (CFC) legislation aims at tax advantages stemming from the deferral of the shareholders' income tax on dividends. If CFC rules apply, the foreign corporation's income is re-classified as domestic income and included in the income of the domestic shareholders pro rata to the shares held. The foreign income is subject to the shareholders' domestic income tax. Foreign taxes may be credited. Some countries, however, only allow the deduction of foreign taxes. The subsequent distribution of the foreign income is, as a rule, not subject to income tax.

In general, CFC legislation applies if the following legal conditions are met. (i) The foreign corporation is controlled by a domestic resident (or sometimes jointly by domestic residents) who owns at least 50% (sometimes 25%) of the shares of the foreign corporation. Within the EU, some countries exclude EU corporations from the scope of CFC legislation. (ii) The foreign company is resident in a low-tax country. This is the case if the foreign effective tax burden is lower than a certain percentage of the domestic corporation tax rate or an explicitly stated tax rate. (iii) The foreign company earns passive income. As a rule, capital income (most prominently interest and royalty income) is deemed to be passive, whereas business activities like manufacturing and commercial transactions are deemed not to be passive.

Within the EU, many smaller Member States have not implemented CFC legislation, e.g. Austria, Cyprus, Ireland, Luxembourg and Malta. The larger Member States, however, rely on CFC legislation, most notably Germany, France, the United Kingdom and Italy. Outside the EU, the U.S. and Japan are prominent examples for countries which have implemented CFC legislation.

2.6.2.2. Thin Capitalization Rules

Thin capitalization (TC) rules aim at excessive shareholder debt financing (internal debt). If the conditions of TC rules are met, the deduction of interest payments which relate to shareholder debt financing is disallowed. Double taxation occurs if the debtor's country of residence disallows the interest payments, whereas the creditor's country of residence taxes the interest income received. If, on the other hand, interest payments are reclassified as dividend, double taxation must not necessarily occur, provided that the creditor's country of residence follows the reclassification of the debtor's country of residence. In this case, the reclassified non-deductible interest payment is taxed as a dividend payment in both countries.

TC legislation usually applies if the following conditions are met. (i) The creditor is a foreign shareholder who owns at least 25% (sometimes 50%) of the equity capital. Some EU Member States address both resident and non-resident shareholders, while other Member States address only non-EU resident shareholders. (ii) The debt-equity ratio is restricted. A debt-equity ratio of 3:1 or 4:1 is common in Member States.

Smaller EU Member States do not apply TC rules, e.g. Cyprus, Estonia, Ireland and Malta. Larger Member States regularly apply TC legislation, e.g. the United Kingdom and France. Outside the EU, again, the U.S. and Japan are prominent examples. Two EU Member States, Italy and Germany, extend the scope of TC legislation to all kinds of debt financing, i.e. internal (shareholder) debt and external debt, e.g. a bank loan. In general, in both countries, deductibility of interest expenses is limited to a certain percentage of an earnings figure (interest stripping rule). Germany disallows the deduction of interest payments exceeding 30% of the earnings before interest, taxes, depreciation and amortization (EBITDA). Excessive interest payments may be carried forward and deducted in following years, as with a loss carry forward, provided that the EBITDA restriction is not applicable in the respective period. The TC legislation of Germany and Italy is not only designed to combat excessive shareholder debt financing (internal debt), but also to fight international tax arbitrage by means of external debt financing.

Reading List Chapter 2

Amatucci, Andrea: International Tax Law, Alphen aan den Rijn, 2006.

Brealey, Richard A.; Myers, Stewart C.: Principles of Corporate Finance, 9th Edition, New York, 2007.

Desai, Mihir A.; Hines, James R.: Evaluating International Tax Reform, in: National Tax Journal 2003, pp. 487-502.

Devereux, Michael P.: Business taxation in a globalized world, in: Oxford Review of Economic Policy 2008, pp. 625–638.

Devereux, Michael P; Griffith, Rachel: Evaluating Tax Policy for Location Decisions, in: International Tax and Public Finance 2003, pp. 107-126.

Frenkel, Jacob A.; Razin, Assaf; Sadka, Efraim: International Taxation in an Integrated World, Cambridge, 1991.

Homburg, Stefan: Competition and Co-ordination in International Capital Income Taxation, FinanzArchiv 1999, pp. 1 – 17.

King, Mervyn A.; Fullerton, Don: The Taxation of Income from Capital; Chicago, 1984.

Kofler, Georg: Indirect Credit versus Exemption: Double Taxation Relief for Intercompany Distributions, in: Bulletin for International Taxation 2012, pp. 77-89

Kruschwitz, Lutz; Löffler, Andreas: Discounted Cash Flow – A Theory of the Valuation of Firms, Chichester, 2006.

Mogdialiani, Franco; Miller, Merton H.: The Cost of Capital, Corporation Finance, and the Theory of Investment, in: American Economic Review 1958, pp. 261-297.

Musgrave, Peggy B. (ed.): Tax Policy in the Global Economy, Cheltenham/ Northhampton, 2002.

Russo, Raffaele (ed.): Fundamentals of International Tax Planning, Amsterdam, 2007.

Schanz, Deborah; Schanz, Sebastian: Business Taxation and Financial Decisions, Heidelberg, 2011.

Sinn, Hans W.: Capital Income Taxation and Resource Allocation, North Holland, Amsterdam, New York, Oxford and Tokio, 1987.

Slemrod, Joel B.: Free Trade Taxation and Protectionist Taxation, in: International Tax and Public Finance 1995, pp. 471-489.

Tanzi, Vito: Taxation in an Integrated World, Washington, 1995.

Vogel, Klaus: Worldwide vs. Source Taxation of Income – A review and reevaluation of arguments (Part I, II, III), in: Intertax 1988, pp. 216-229; pp. 310-320; pp. 393-402.

3. International Corporate Tax Planning

3.1. Tasks of International Corporate Tax Planning

Multinational corporate groups engage in tax planning to increase after-tax cash flows and the groups' market value. In the first place, international tax planning aims at avoiding legal double taxation. In second place, international tax planning focuses on tax arbitrage. Avoidance of double taxation is the first priority of international tax planning because double taxation of profits severely reduces a multinational group's profitability. A multinational group's legal structure responds to double taxation problems and reflects the international allocation of taxing rights. Nevertheless, intra-group transactions may give rise to double taxation as tax bases may overlap when different countries apply different rules to determine the tax base (e.g. when assessing transfer prices).

International Tax Arbitrage

International tax arbitrage aims at cash flow and interest advantages by exploiting differences in taxes levied, in tax bases and in statutory tax rates across countries. Capital markets monitor a multinational group's effective tax rate reported in the financial accounts, i.e. the ratio of tax expenses to pre-tax profits, and thus foster international tax arbitrage. International tax arbitrage comes in many forms. Multinational groups decide on investment locations, the legal form of foreign investments, acquisition of foreign companies, financing and profit distribution, the allocation of ownership rights, and the structure of intra-group asset transfers. All these decisions influence the overall tax burden of a multinational group.

In international taxation, the fact that a corporation is a distinct entity is the most important legal construct. Setting up a foreign corporation provides access to the foreign corporation tax system and is the usual means to engage in international tax arbitrage. Pass-through taxation is far less important. Yet, pass-through taxation may come into play if foreign investments are carried out through a (foreign) partnership or branch (permanent establishment). In case of a partnership, as a rule, the domestic corporation is taxed on its share in the partnerships profits and losses. A foreign permanent establishment is not considered a legally distinct entity and is thus also subject to pass-through taxation, i.e. the profits and losses of the permanent establishment are regarded as taxable income of the domestic corporation.

Restrictions and Frictions

Legal restrictions reduce the room for maneuver of tax planning schemes which aim at exploiting an international tax differential. Specific tax rules may be targeted, for example, at a group's transfer prices, a company's retained earnings or leverage and in effect reduce or even eliminate expected tax savings.

International tax planning faces economic frictions in terms of tax planning costs. The costs of tax planning entail indirect as well as direct costs. Among the direct costs are the fees for legal advice and the taxpayers cost to comply with the tax law, e.g. by preparing tax accounts and income tax statements. Indirect costs are incurred if tax efficient structures of a group's transactions fall short of the structures chosen by the group in the absence of taxes. Efficient tax planning does not solely aim at minimizing the amount of taxes paid but takes into account the non-tax cost of tax planning as well as the tax risks involved.

3.2. Investment Decisions

3.2.1. Legal Form

In terms of the legal form of foreign investment, corporate investors have the choice between a permanent establishment and a subsidiary. The permanent establishment is legally not separated from the investor and pass-through taxation applies. Conversely, the subsidiary is a distinct entity in legal terms.

Permanent Establishment

If a corporation chooses a permanent establishment, the source country where the permanent establishment is located has the right to tax the income earned through (attributed to) the permanent establishment (Art. 5 and Art. 7 OECD-MT). The respective profits are subject to corporation tax in the source country (limited tax liability). As a rule, withholding taxes are not levied in the source country upon repatriation of the profits of the permanent establishment.

The residence country of the corporation may have the right to tax business income derived from the foreign permanent establishment (unlimited tax liability). Yet, many double taxation treaties, among them the majority of German treaties, exempt such foreign profits from domestic taxation.

Subsidiary

If the corporation establishes a foreign corporation, the foreign corporation is a separate legal entity subject to unlimited tax liability in the foreign country. If profits are distributed, both the source country (limited tax liability of the investor) and the residence country (unlimited tax liability of the investor) are entitled to tax the dividends. Foreign withholding taxes burdened on dividends can be credited against the domestic corporation's tax liability. Germany exempts inter-corporate dividends, but charges 5% of the dividends as non-deductible business expenses to corporation tax and to local trade tax.[14]

Within the EU, withholding taxes are limited by the PSD. The PSD covers inter-corporate dividends of European corporations if they are resident in the EU and the shareholding exceeds 10%. Withholding taxes are disallowed in the source country. The residence country of the corporate investors has to account for double taxation by using either the exemption or the credit method. The classification of 5% of the dividends as non-deductible business expenses in Germany, France and some other European countries is permitted by the PSD. As a result, European corporate groups do not face withholding taxes on dividend income.

If the corporation distributes the foreign profits, i.e. the foreign subsidiaries dividends or the profits earned in foreign permanent establishments, the corporations' shareholders are taxed upon the dividends received. If the corporations' shareholders are German individuals, dividends are either subject to a final withholding tax of 25% (shareholding is held as private asset) or 60% of the dividend is taxed as ordinary income subject to the progressive income tax rate schedule (i.e., 40% of the dividend is tax-free if the shareholding is a business asset). In both cases, foreign withholding taxes are creditable against the investors' domestic income tax liability.

Permanent Establishment versus Subsidiary

When choosing between a foreign subsidiary and a foreign permanent establishment, the local profits taxes are irrelevant. Corporate investors are either subject to unlimited tax liability (subsidiary) or subject to limited tax liability (permanent establishment). In both cases, in the foreign country the corporation tax rate applies.

Example (3.1): G Corporation is located in the EU Member State G and wholly owned by an individual who is resident in EU Member State G. G Corporation considers investing in Member State F through a permanent establishment or through a wholly owned subsidiary which immediately distributes its profits. G Corporations profits (cash flows) are taxed at $\tau_G = 30\%$. The individual shareholder is taxed at $\tau_D = 25\%$ on dividend income. The corporation tax rate in country F amounts to $\tau_F = 25\%$. Country F levies a withholding tax on dividends of 15% (according to the double tax treaty). Country G exempts foreign profits as well as inter-corporate dividends, but taxes 5% of the dividends as non-deductible business expense.

14 See Sec. 8b Para. 1 Corporation Tax Act (KStG).

			Permanent Establishment	Subsidiary
	G Corporation			
1	Profit before taxes in F		100.00	100.00
2	Corporation tax in F	25% · (1)	25.00	25.00
3	Profit after taxes in F	(1) – (2)	75.00	75.00
4	Withholding tax			0.00
5	Net dividends	(1) – (2) – (4)		75.00
6	Corporate income in G	5% · (3)	Exemption	3.75
7	Corporation tax in G	30% · (6)		1.13
8	Profit distribution	(1)-(2)-(4)-(7)	75.00	73.87
	Individual shareholder			
9	Dividend	(8)	75.00	73.87
10	Tax on dividends	25% · (8)	18.75	18.47
11	Net cash flow	(9) – (10)	56.25	55.40

In case of a permanent establishment, G Corporation's foreign profits are tax-exempt in country G on the corporate level under the double tax treaty. If G Corporation chooses to establish a foreign subsidiary, the repatriation of the foreign profits triggers foreign withholding taxes on dividends which may be reduced in amount by a double taxation treaty. As G Corporation holds 100% of the shares in the subsidiary, the PSD applies and the withholding tax is reduced to zero. In country G, 95% of the dividends received, are tax-free. An amount of 5% of the dividends triggers corporation taxes. If the tax law is the only consideration, G Corporation will choose to invest in country F through a permanent establishment.

Under the assumptions of the Example (3.1), a permanent establishment is preferred over a subsidiary because the distribution of foreign profits is not reduced by additional taxes in the residence country of the corporate investor. The tax advantage of the permanent establishment increases, if the foreign (non-EU) country levies withholding taxes on dividends. Withholding taxes cannot be credited in the corporation's residence country because foreign dividends are tax-free there. Shareholder taxation does not affect the corporation´s decision with respect to the legal form of the foreign investment.

3.2.2. Investment Location

Taxes, among other economic factors, are an important factor in investment location decisions. The tax burden of an investment is basically determined by both the tax rate and the tax base. At first glance, a high tax rate in a location seems to be unfavorable. In the case of a marginal investment, however, the opposite may be true. If the investment is tax-advantageous with respect to the tax base, a high statutory tax rate translates in high tax savings due to the favorable tax base. Prominent examples are accelerated depreciation or immediate deduction of the investment outlay.

On the other hand, the higher the rate of return on the investment, the more advantageous are low statutory tax rates. The positive effect of a favorable tax base remains constant irrespective of the profitability, whereas the negative effect of a high statutory tax rate on profits becomes more important when taxable profits rise. Because many countries have followed a tax policy of tax-rate-cut-cum-base-broadening in the past, profitable investments may be attracted by a low tax rate. On the other hand, marginal investments may suffer from tax base broadening thus reducing the amount of invested capital.

Marginal Investments

Investors who already invest in different locations face the choice of where to locate additional investments. In such a setting, the tax effect on marginal investments matters. To illustrate the choice of the location for a marginal investment, assume a corporation which decides upon a marginal investment to be either carried out in the home country or in a foreign country.

Example (3.2): G Corporation is resident in country G. G Corporation invests equity capital of 100 in a self-created intangible asset (development costs). G Corporation is considering investing either in country G or in the foreign country F via a permanent establishment. In both countries, the same pre-tax cash flows are expected. The capital market interest rate is i = 10%. G Corporation is subject to limited tax liability in country F and taxed at a corporation tax rate of τ_F = 20%. In country F, the investment outlay is capitalized and depreciated straight-line over a period of two years, whereas in country G the investment outlay is immediately expensed. The foreign business income is tax-exempt in country G. Individual income taxes are ignored (τ_{FI} = 0%, i_τ = 10%).

t	0	1	2
I_0	-100.00		
CF_t		60.00	55.00
D_t		50.00	50.00
CF_t - D_t		10.00	5.00
$T_t = \tau_F \cdot (CF_t - D_t)$		2.00	1.00
$I_0 + CF_t - T_t$	-100.00	58.00	54.00
NPV after taxes	$C_0^\tau = -100 + \frac{(60-2)}{1.10} + \frac{(55-1)}{1.10^2} = -2.64$		

If the investment is located in country F, its NPV is negative because the after-tax rate of return is lower than the market interest rate of 10%.

If the investment is located in country G, G Corporation as a tax payer with unlimited tax liability faces a corporation tax rate of $\tau_C = 40\%$. An immediate loss offset is available.

t	0	1	2
I_0	-100.00		
CF_t		60.00	55.00
D_t	-100.00		
CF_t - D_t	-100.00	60.00	55.00
$T_t = \tau_C \cdot (CF_t - D_t)$	-40.00	24.00	22.00
$I_0 + CF_t - T_t$	-60.00	36.00	33.00
NPV after taxes	$C_0^\tau = -100 + 40 + \frac{(60-24)}{1.10} + \frac{(55-22)}{1.10^2} = 0$		

The investment's NPV is zero. The investor is indifferent between the real investment in country G and a capital market investment at 10%. The favorable tax base effect (classification of the investment outlay as immediately deductible expenses and immediate loss offset) outweighs the unfavorable tax rate effect ($\tau_C = 40\%$ in relation to $\tau_F = 20\%$).

In the Example (3.2), country G in effect grants a tax deduction on the investment outlay. The tax savings related to the investment outlay are thus front-loaded. The positive timing effect generated by the tax base outweighs the negative tax rate effect. As a result, the marginal investment is better off in tax terms if located in country G.

Profitable Investments

Investors who face the decision where to locate a profitable investment primarily react to differences in statutory tax rates. Consider the investment in Example (3.2), but assume that the pre-tax cash flows are higher, which renders the investment profitable before taxes. Because the investment has a positive pre-tax NPV, the low corporation tax rate in country F favors the investment.

Example (3.3): The assumptions of Example (3.2) apply. In case of an investment in country F, G Corporation faces a profit tax rate of $\tau_F = 20\%$ and has to capitalize the investment.

t	0	1	2
I_0	-100.00		
CF_t		90.00	82.50
D_t		50.00	50.00
$CF_t - D_t$		40.00	32.50
$T_t = \tau_C \cdot (CF_t - D_t)$		8.00	6.50
$I_0 + CF_t - T_t$	-100.00	82.00	76.00
NPV after taxes	$C_0^\tau = -100 + \frac{(90-8)}{1.10} + \frac{(82.50-6.50)}{1.10^2} = +37.36$		

If G Corporation decides to locate the investment in country G, the higher tax rate of $\tau_C = 40\%$ applies and immediate tax-deductibility of the investment outlay is available.

t	0	1	2
I_0	-100.00		
CF_t		90.00	82.50
D_t	-100.00		
CF_t - D_t	-100.00	90.00	82.50
$T_t = \tau_C \cdot (CF_t - D_t)$	-40.00	36.00	33.00
$I_0 + CF_t$ - T_t	-60.00	54.00	49.50
NPV after taxes	$C_0^\tau = -100 + 40 + \frac{(90-36)}{1.10} + \frac{(82.50-33)}{1.10^2} = +30.00$		

The location of the investment in country F is preferred over the investment's location in country G. The low profit tax rate works in favor of country F.

In Example (3.3), the tax rate effect is decisive, whereas the tax base is of minor importance. The higher tax rate hits the positive NPV while the timing effect caused by the tax base remains unchanged. Due to these effects, location decisions on profitable investments are driven by differences in the location's statutory tax rate.

3.2.3. Acquisitions

Companies do not only transfer capital to foreign countries to invest in new projects (greenfield investments). Capital is also transferred via the acquisition of the ownership rights in foreign firms. An acquisition does not immediately affect the actual investments of the acquired firms. The transfer of ownership rights is advantageous if new owners attach a higher value to the firm than the former owners. New owners may be more production efficient or may have advantages in the sales market. Efficiency advantages may also be related to firm-specific intangibles (as brands or know-how) which can more efficiently be exploited by the buyer when combined with the acquired firm.

Price Effects of Taxes

The corporate profit tax burden is determined by the tax law of the country where the target corporation is located. The tax burden on distributed profits depends on the tax law of the country where the owner of the shares is resident. Corporations may be more valuable for certain owners due to tax characteristics. Tax efficient buyers pay a higher price for the target company than tax inefficient buyers.

To assess the tax effect on the maximum price the buyer is willing to pay and the minimum price the seller demands, assume a target T Corporation located in country T, a buyer B Corporation and a seller S Corporation, both corporations located in countries B and S respectively. The shareholders of B Corporation and S Corporation are natural persons and are resident in the same country as B Corporation and S Corporation. In order to isolate the tax effects, any economic rent stemming from combining the target's assets with the buyers assets is ignored, even though that benefit may be the driving force of an acquisition.

The Seller's Minimum Price

T Corporation's profit (cash flow) after taxes is risk-free and constant over time. T Corporation distributes its after-tax profit to S Corporation:

(3.1) $$DIV_T = PR_T \cdot (1 - \tau_T).$$

PR_T and DIV_T denote the pre-tax cash flow and the dividend respectively, and τ_T is the profit tax rate of T Corporation. Dividends received by S Corporation are not taxed. However, individual shareholders of S Corporation pay income taxes on the dividend distribution of S Corporation. The after-tax dividend received by S Corporation's shareholders amounts to

(3.2) $$DIV_S^\tau = DIV_T \cdot (1 - \tau_{D,S})$$

where $\tau_{D,S}$ denotes the personal income tax rate on dividends of shareholders resident in country S.

If T Corporation is terminated at time $t = n$, the after-tax value of T Corporation at time $t = 0$ amounts to

(3.3) $$V_S^\tau = DIV_S^\tau \cdot R(i, \tau_{I,S}, n) = PR_T \cdot (1 - \tau_T) \cdot (1 - \tau_{D,S}) \cdot R(i, \tau_{I,S}, n)$$

with the annuity factor $R(i, \tau_{I,S}, n)$.[15] The variable i denotes the market interest rate, $\tau_{I,S}$ denominates the individual income tax rate on interest income received in country S, and n indicates time. For the sake of simplicity, equity contributions to T Corporation and the resulting acquisition cost of S Corporation's shareholding in T Corporation are ignored.

S Corporation is indifferent between selling the shares and holding the shares in T Corporation if the after-tax revenue from selling the shares equals the after-tax NPV of holding the shares:

(3.4) $$P_S \cdot (1 - \tau_{D,S}) = V_S^\tau$$

[15] The annuity factor amounts to $R(i, \tau_{I,S}, n) = \frac{1}{i \cdot (1 - \tau_{I,S})} \cdot \left\{1 - \frac{1}{[1 + i \cdot (1 - \tau_{I,S})]^n}\right\}$.

where P_S denotes the minimum price which is required by S Corporation. The left hand side of equation (3.4) indicates the shareholders' net cash flow from the sale of the shareholding in T Corporation. S Corporation's gain upon the sale of the shares in T Corporation is not taxed. S Corporation distributes the proceeds from the sale as dividends to its shareholders. The right hand side of equation (3.4) represents the NPV of the dividend stream generated by T Corporation where the shareholding is not sold. Equation (3.5) gives S Corporation's minimum price

$$(3.5) \qquad P_S = \frac{V_S^\tau}{1-\tau_{D,S}} = PR \cdot (1-\tau_T) \cdot R(i, \tau_{I,S}, n).$$

The seller's price exceeds the after-tax value of T Corporation at time $t = 0$ (equation (3.3)) because the gain upon the sale of the shares is burdened with dividend taxes.

The Buyer's Maximum Price

B Corporation, the bidder for T Corporation's shares, is not liable to corporation tax on dividends received from T Corporation, but takes into account individual income taxes of its shareholders resident in country B. The shareholders' after-tax dividend amounts to

$$(3.6) \qquad DIV_B^\tau = DIV_T \cdot (1-\tau_{D,B})$$

where $\tau_{D,B}$ denotes the individual income tax rate on dividend income of shareholders resident in country B. B Corporation determines the after-tax value of T Corporation at time $t = 0$

$$(3.7) \qquad \begin{aligned} V_B^\tau &= DIV_B^\tau \cdot R(i, \tau_{I,B}, n) \\ &= PR_T \cdot (1-\tau_T) \cdot (1-\tau_{D,B}) \cdot R(i, \tau_{I,B}, n) \end{aligned}$$

with the annuity factor $R(i, \tau_{I,B}, n)$ taking into account that interest income in country B is subject to the individual income tax at the rate $\tau_{I,B}$.

B Corporation's shareholders contribute equity capital in the amount of the acquisition price P_B to finance the acquisition. The equity contribution increases the book value of their shareholding in B Corporation. In return to their equity contribution, the shareholders receive a stream of dividends. At time $t = n$ the book value of the shares in B Corporation is written down to its market value of zero (i.e. the tax book value is reduced by the amount P_B) because T Corporation is terminated at time $t = n$ and the shareholders do not receive dividends thereafter $t > n$. B Corporation determines the maximum price for the shares in T Corporation taking into account the after-tax value of T Corporation's dividends plus the shareholders' tax savings with respect to the written down tax book value of the shares in B Corporation

$$(3.8) \qquad P_B = V_B^\tau + \tau_{CG,B} \cdot q(i, \tau_{I,B}, n) \cdot P_B.$$

The right hand side of equation (3.8) indicates the shareholders' net cash flow when buying the shareholding in T Corporation plus the NPV of the income tax saving from writing down the tax book value of the shares in B Corporation. The term $\tau_{CG,B}$ denotes the individual capital gains tax rate in country B and the term $q(i, \tau_{I,B}, n)$ denotes the after-tax present value factor for $t = n$. Equation (3.9) gives the buyer's maximum price

(3.9) $$P_B = \frac{V_B^\tau}{1-\tau_{CG,B} \cdot q(i,\tau_{I,B},n)} = \frac{PR_T \cdot (1-\tau_T) \cdot (1-\tau_{D,B}) \cdot R(i,\tau_{I,B},n)}{1-\tau_{CG,B} \cdot q(i,\tau_{I,B},n)}.$$

B Corporation's maximum price exceeds the after-tax value of T Corporation (V_B^τ) because the price takes into account the income tax savings of the shareholders at time $t = n$.

Tax Wedge

Taxes may drive a wedge between the buyer's maximum price and the seller's minimum price. The comparison of equation (3.5) and equation (3.9) reveals that the after-tax value of the target corporation depends on the individual income tax rates on dividends and, via the annuity factor, on the individual income tax rates on interest income. Moreover, the buyer's maximum price is affected by the income tax rate on capital gains and a timing effect related to capital gains taxation.

Assuming a uniform individual income tax rate on dividends and capital gains in country B ($\tau_{D,B} = \tau_{CG,B}$) and immediate expensing of the equity contribution to B Corporation, $q(i, \tau_{I,B}, n) = 1$, leads to

(3.10) $$P_B = \frac{V_B^\tau}{1-\tau_{CG,B}} = PR_T \cdot (1 - \tau_T) \cdot R(i, \tau_{I,B}, n).$$

The maximum price depends on the target corporation's net profit distribution and the annuity factor. However, the minimum and maximum prices will differ if the individual income tax rates on interest income are different.

Price effects of taxes completely vanish if individual income taxation is ignored. The maximum price then equals the minimum price:

(3.11) $$P_B = P_S = V_B^\tau = V_S^\tau = PR_T \cdot (1 - \tau_T) \cdot R(i, n)$$

The price identity indicates that taxes do not distort the acquisition. Seller and buyer discount the same net cash flow at the same market interest rate. These conditions may be relevant if publicly held corporations are involved in a share deal. Withholding taxes are often not levied on inter-corporate dividends (as it is the case under the PSD) or are significantly reduced by double tax treaties. Inter-corporate dividends and corporations' capital gains upon the sale of shares are usually tax-free. Hence, corporate buyers and corporate sellers of shares take only the target's profit taxes into account.

Individual income taxation may be ignored because the corporations engaged in the share deal do not have sufficient information about the income tax position of their shareholders. Moreover, publicly held corporations face a pre-tax market interest rate which represents the required rate of return. Under these conditions, share prices do not reflect individual income taxes on investments.

Example (3.4): T Corporation earns a profit (cash flow) per year of $PR = 100$ for $n = 10$ years. In year $t = 10$, T Corporation is liquidated. The market interest rate amounts to i = 5%. The table displays the tax rate data, the discount factors, the dividends, the value of the target, the buyer's maximum price and the seller's minimum price.

	T Corporation	S Corporation	B Corporation
$\tau_{D,*}$ (%)		20.00	30.00
$\tau_{I,*}$ (%)		20.00	30.00
$\tau_{CG,B}$ (%)			30.00
τ_T (%)	25.00		
$q(5\%, \tau_{I,B}, 10)$			0.71
$R(5\%, \tau_{I,*}, 10)$		8.11	8.32
PR_T	100.00		
D_T	75.00		
D_*^τ		60.00	52.50
V_*^τ		486.65	436.62
P_*		608.32	554.56

S Corporation's minimum price $P_S = 608.32$ exceeds B Corporation's maximum price $P_B = 554.56$, indicating that taxes drive a wedge between the minimum and the maximum price. Shareholder taxation drives the result. Ignoring shareholder taxation with respect to dividends, capital gains and interest income leads to $P_S = P_B = 579.13$.

Tax Planning

Going beyond the simplified assumptions of the above analysis, multinational groups make use of tax planning schemes in order to reduce the overall tax burden of the target company after the acquisition. If the target company faces high profit taxes, the acquiring company may increase its leverage after the acquisition with internal or external loans reducing its profits taxes through tax-deductible interest payments. Once the target company has become a part of the acquiring group, transfer pricing may be employed to reduce its profits taxes. If, on the other hand, the target company is low-taxed, the buyer may reduce its leverage and shift profits to it through transfer pricing in order to reduce the overall tax burden of the group.

Tax savings due to post-acquisition tax planning increase the target company's net cash flow and thus effects on the value of the target's shares for the buyer. Tax planning through debt financing and transfer pricing is only useful in cases of cross-border acquisitions where tax rate differentials are exploited.

3.2.4. Allocation of Ownership Rights

A corporation carrying out an investment usually holds the ownership rights of the assets purchased and used in the production process. Yet, the ownership rights to assets of a corporation can be assigned to an affiliated corporation located in another country. The corporation using the assets has to pay a user fee to the corporation owning them. A common example for the split of ownership rights and the use of assets is a leasing contract where the lessor owns the asset while the lessee uses the asset and pays a leasing fee.

In the area of international tax planning, the split of ownership rights and the use of assets are especially important in case of valuable intellectual property (IP) generated by research and development, e.g. patents, trademarks and technical know-how.

Research and Development

Research and development (R&D) investments are of critical importance for many multinational companies, e.g. chemical companies, pharmaceutical companies, or software companies. These companies invest large amounts in R&D. From a non-tax perspective, the location of IP primarily depends on the legal protection a country offers for IP rights, e.g. duration of patents and legal enforcement. From a tax viewpoint, intellectual property should be owned by companies located in a country levying low taxes on the income it generates. Conversely, expenses incurred by the production of IP should be tax-deductible at a high tax rate. In general, R&D investments generate assets which are not capitalized in the tax accounts. Investment outlays immediately reduce the taxable profit. Companies have an incentive to combine low tax payments on profits with high tax savings related to expenses.

A multinational group faces the choice either to perform R&D activities by a company to own the IP created (R&D Company) or to perform R&D activities on a contract basis on behalf of another group company to own the new IP (IP Company).

R&D Company Creates and Owns IP

If the company carrying out the investment and owning the resulting IP (R&D Company) is located in a high-tax country and earns sufficient profits, R&D expenses trigger immediate tax savings at the high profits tax rate τ_H. Profits from using or selling IP are subject to the same high tax rate. The NPV of the R&D investment amounts to

$$C_0^\tau = -I_0 \cdot (1-\tau_H) + \sum_{t=1}^{n} CF_t \cdot (1-\tau_H)(1+i_\tau)^{-t} \\ = (1-\tau_H) \cdot [-I_0 + \sum_{t=1}^{n} CF_t \cdot (1+i_\tau)^{-t}] \quad (3.12)$$

where i_τ denotes the multinational company's discount rate. The investment outlay at time $t = 0$ is immediately expensed and subsequent cash flows are fully taxable (fully tax-deductible if negative). In effect, the investment's NPV before profits taxes is taxed at the statutory tax rate.

R&D Company Creates IP and IP Company owns IP

If the IP Company owns the IP and pays a fee for the services provided by the R&D Company, namely the creation of intellectual property, the fee covers the production cost of the R&D Company plus a profit mark-up which has to conform to the arm's length principle. The IP Company uses or sells the IP and earns a profit. IP Company's profit is taxed at tax rate $\tau_L < \tau_H$. The NPV of the R&D investment consists of the NPV of the R&D Company carrying out contract research plus the NPV of the IP Company.

Assume for the sake of simplicity, the production of the IP takes place at time $t = 0$ and subsequent cash flows stem from selling the IP at time $t = 0$ to the IP Company. The profit of the R&D Company equals the profit mark-up if the IP price covers the production cost plus the profit mark-up. R&D Company's NPV under contract research amounts to

$$C_0^{\tau,R\&D} = (1-\tau_H) \cdot [-I_0 + I_0 \cdot (1+m)] = (1-\tau_H) \cdot m \cdot I_0 \quad (3.13)$$

with m denoting the profit mark-up. Assuming that IP Company is allowed to immediately deduct the payments made to R&D Company, the IP Company's NPV amounts to

$$C_0^{\tau,IP} = (1-\tau_L) \cdot [-I_0 \cdot (1+m) + \sum_{t=1}^{n} CF_t \cdot (1+i_\tau)^{-t}]. \quad (3.14)$$

Both companies' pre-tax NPVs are taxed at the respective corporation tax rate. The overall after-tax NPV of both companies amounts to:

$$(3.15) \qquad C_0^{\tau,R\&D} + C_0^{\tau,IP} = m \cdot I_0 \cdot (\tau_L - \tau_H) + (1-\tau_L) \cdot [-I_0 + \textstyle\sum_{t=1}^{n} CF_t \cdot (1+i_\tau)^{-t}].$$

The tax effects are determined by the tax burdened on the cash flow and the tax rate differential with respect to the profit mark-up.

Comparison of Net Present Values

In order to identify a possible tax advantage of interposing the IP Company, the NPVs of the investment alternatives are compared by deducting the NPV if the R&D Company creates and owns the IP equation (3.12) from the NPV where R&D Company creates the IP and IP Company owns the IP equation (3.15):

$$(3.16) \qquad C_0^{\tau,R\&D} + C_0^{\tau,IP} - C_0^{\tau} = (\tau_L - \tau_H) \cdot I_0 \cdot (1+m) + (\tau_H - \tau_L) \cdot \textstyle\sum_{t=1}^{n} CF_t \cdot (1+i_\tau)^{-t}.$$

The first term on the right hand side of equation (3.16) denotes the tax savings of incurring expenses in the high-tax country as well as the net tax burden on the profit mark-up of R&D Company. The second term denotes the tax savings with respect to the cash flows generated by the low-taxed IP Company.

Example (3.5): R&D Company is resident in country C and considers an investment in R&D. The profit tax rate in country C amounts to τ_H = 30%. The market interest rate at which C Company discounts its cash flows amounts to i_τ = 5%. The investment outlay is immediately expensed. An immediate loss offset is available.

t	0	1	2
I_0	-100.00		
CF_t		60.00	55.00
$T_t = \tau_H \cdot CF_t$	-30.00	18.00	16.50
$I_0 + CF_t - T_t$	-70.00	42.00	38.50
NPV after taxes	$C_0^{\tau} = -100 + 30 + \frac{(60-18)}{1.05} + \frac{(55-16.50)}{1.05^2} = 4.92$		

Alternatively, C Corporation might consider carrying out contract research for IP Corporation, a 100% subsidiary resident in the low-tax country IP, facing a profit tax rate of τ_L = 10%. Profit distributions of IP Corporation are tax-free when received by C Corporation.

The profit mark-up m based on C Corporation's investment outlay is at arm's length and amounts to m = 5%, which equals the market interest rate.

t	0	1	2
I_0	-100.00		
$I_0 + m \cdot I_0$	+105.00		
$T_t = \tau_H \cdot m \cdot I_0$	1.50		
$m \cdot I_0 - T_t$	3.50		
NPV C Corporation	$C_0^{\tau,R\&D} = 3.50$		
$I_0 + m \cdot I_0$	-105.00		
CF_t		60.00	55.00
$T_t = \tau_L * CF_t$	-10.50	6.00	5.50
$I_0 + m \cdot I_0 + CF_t - T_t$	-94.50	54.00	49.50
NPV IP Corporation	$C_0^{\tau,IP} = -105 + 10.50 + \frac{(60-6)}{1.05} + \frac{(55-5.50)}{1.05^2} = 1.83$		
Overall NPV	$C_0^{\tau,R\&D} + C_0^{\tau,IP} = 3.50 + 1.83 = 5.33$		

The interposition of IP Corporation increases the investment's NPV by 0.41 ($C_0^{\tau,R\&D} + C_0^{\tau,IP} - C_0^{\tau} = 5.33 - 4.92 = 0.41$). According to equation (3.4), there is a negative effect due to the tax rate differential $\tau_L - \tau_H = -20\%$ related to the investment outlay and to the profit mark-up ($-21 = -20\% \cdot 105$). A positive effect due to the tax rate differential $\tau_H - \tau_L = 20\%$ is related to the pre-tax NPV of the investment's cash flows ($21.41 = 20\% \cdot 107.03$). The overall tax effect amounts to 0.41 (= 21.41 – 21). The interposition of IP Company reduces the tax savings in time t = 0, but increases the after-tax cash flows in time t = 1 and time t = 2.

Tax Conditions for Interposing an IP Company

An IP company should be located in countries which provide favorable tax conditions for the creation and exploitation of intellectual property rights. The relevant tax factors for interposing an IP company are a low profits tax rate in the residence country of the IP Company and, eventually, tax incentives for the creation of intellectual property, e.g. R&D tax credits, in the country where R&D actually takes place. Profits distributed by an IP Company should be received tax-free by the parent company. IP Companies may be subject to CFC rules in which case higher profits taxes apply, eliminating their tax rate advantage.

License fees paid by group companies using intellectual property of an IP company should not be subjected to withholding taxes in order to avoid excess credit situation for a low-taxed IP company. Within the EU, withholding taxes are not allowed to be levied by the source country if the Interest and Royalties Directive applies.

3.2.5. Loss Compensation

Tax loss compensation ensures that the tax base reflects all expenses incurred to perform the investment, independent of cash flow patterns. If losses are tax-deductible, the investor receives a tax benefit when the losses are incurred. This benefit increases the investment's cash flow and NPV. In some circumstances, losses may only be deducted from future profits (loss carry-forward), generating future tax savings. The loss carry-forward also entails positive effects on the investments cash flow. However, it is not interest bearing, the investor suffers from negative timing effects, reducing the investments' NPV. In a cross border setting, both effects depend on the loss offset rules applicable in the source country and in the residence country.

Cash Flow Effect

Under accrual accounting, tax losses (a negative tax base) are not identical with negative cash flows. A negative tax base may occur because tax depreciation exceeds revenues (cash inflows). A corporation carrying out an additional investment may be in a position to offset losses suffered from the additional investment with profits from other activities. The resulting tax savings of the corporations have their origin in the additional investment and should be allocated to this investment. An immediate tax deduction increases the investment's after-tax cash flow and NPV. A loss carry-back allows deducting losses from profits of previous tax years. The loss carry-back may also result in an immediate tax refund. However, a loss carry-back is often not available or is severely restricted by time and by amount.

Example (3.6): C Corporation invests 100 in an asset with a useful life of two years (the tax depreciation is 50 each year). C Corporation is in an overall profit situation and is taxed at 30%. Net cash flows are discounted at the net interest rate $i_\tau = 7\%$.

t	0	1	2
I_0	-100.00		
CF_t		0.00	119.20
D_t		50.00	50.00
CF_t - D_t		-50.00	69.20
T_t		15.00	-20.76
$I_0 + CF_t - T_t$	-100.00	15.00	98.44
NPV after taxes	$C_0^\tau = -100 + \frac{0.00 - 0.3 \cdot (-50.00)}{1.07} + \frac{119.20 - 0.3 \cdot 69.20}{1.07^2} = 0.00$		

The tax savings at $t = 1$ increase the investment's cash flow. The after-tax NPV of zero indicates a marginal investment. The tax burden increases, if C Corporation is not able to deduct the loss.

t	0	1	2
I_0	-100.00		
CF_t		0.00	119.20
D_t		50.00	50.00
CF_t - D_t		-50.00	69.20
T_t		0.00	-20.76
$I_0 + CF_t - T_t$	-100.00	0.00	98.44
NPV after taxes	$C_0^\tau = -100 + \frac{0.00 - 0.3 \cdot 0.00}{1.07} + \frac{119.20 - 0.3 \cdot 69.20}{1.07^2} = -14.02$		

C Corporation is taxed on a total profit of 69.20 although the undiscounted sum of the investment's pre-tax cash flows amounts only to 19.20 (= - 100 + 119.20). The investment's after-tax cash flow decreases and the NPV is negative because the loss at $t = 1$ is not deducted.

Under the residence principle, a foreign permanent establishment´s loss has to be accounted for in the residence country. In the residence country of the parent company the foreign loss is included in the company´s worldwide income. As a result, an immediate and unrestricted loss offset is available if the parent company is in an overall profit position. If a residence country, however, exempts foreign profits from domestic income tax, foreign losses may be excluded as well. The cash flow effect then depends on the investor's tax position in the source country, where losses may not be deductible.

In case of a foreign subsidiary, losses do not reduce the parent company's taxable income. Losses have to be accounted for in the residence country of the foreign subsidiary. Pooling foreign losses with domestic profits is impossible. The same is true for domestic losses and foreign profits, irrespective of the profit distribution policy of the foreign subsidiary. Foreign retained profits are shielded from the domestic base. Foreign inter-corporate dividends are tax-free and thus not available for loss offset. Given the restrictions on loss transfer, foreign as well as domestic losses may be final, resulting in negative cash flow effects.

Timing Effect

Losses which cannot be used in the fiscal year they were incurred may be deductible from profits in subsequent years (loss carry-forward). The loss carry-forward is usually restricted by time and may be restricted by amount. Restrictions on loss offset entail negative timing effects. Losses which are deducted from the tax base in subsequent years reduce the remaining loss carry-forward:

$$(3.17) \qquad LCF_t = LCF_{t-1} - LS_t$$

where LCF_t denotes the loss carry-forward at time t and LS_t represents the amount of losses deducted from the tax base at time t. With the tax base defined as cash flow minus depreciation ($CF_t - D_t$) and taking into account the loss carry-forward, the tax payment at time t is defined as:

$$(3.18) \qquad \begin{array}{ll} T_t = \tau_{RI} \cdot (CF_t - D_t - LS_t) & \text{if } CF_t - D_t - LS_t > 0 \\ T_t = 0 & \text{if } CF_t - D_t \leq 0 \end{array}$$

The loss carry-forward negatively impacts on the NPV of investments because tax savings from loss deduction are deferred.

Example (3.7): A subsidiary resident in country F faces a corporation tax rate of $\tau_F = 19\%$. The investment outlay of 60 is depreciated over three years on a straight-line basis. The loss carry-forward is restricted to five years. In each year a maximum of 50% of the initial loss is tax-deductible if the subsidiary generates sufficient profits. The subsidiary discounts its cash flows at an interest rate of 10%.

t	0	1	2	3
I_0	-60.00			
CF_t		-100.00	100.00	95.00
D_t		20.00	20.00	20.00
CF_t - D_t		-120.00	80.00	75.00
LS_t		-	60.00	60.00
LCF_t		120.00	60.00	0.00
$T_t = \tau_F \cdot (CF_t - D_t - LS_t)$		0.00	3.80	2.85
$I_0 + CF_t - T_t$	-60.00	-100.00	96.20	92.15
NPV after taxes	$C_0^\tau = -60 - \frac{100}{1.1} + \frac{100 - 3.80}{1.1^2} + \frac{95 - 2.85}{1.1^3} = -2.17$			

Although all losses can be deducted from taxable income, the restrictions on loss compensation disadvantage the investment. The investor suffers from a negative timing effect. The negative effect of restrictions on loss compensation disappears if an immediate loss offset is available.

t	0	1	2	3
I_0	-60.00			
CF_t		-100.00	100.00	95.00
D_t		20.00	20.00	20.00
$CF_t - D_t$		-120.00	80.00	75.00
T_t		-22.80	15.20	14.25
$CF_t - T_t$	-60.00	-77.20	84.80	80.75
NPV after taxes	$C_0^T = -60 \frac{-100+22.8}{1.1} + \frac{100-15.2}{1.1^2} + \frac{95-14.25}{1.1^3} = 0.57$			

Due to the immediate loss offset, the after-tax NPV of the investment is positive. Compared to the case with restrictions on loss deduction, the investment's NPV increases by 2.74 (= 0.57 – (–2.17)).

Taking immediate loss compensation as a benchmark, the loss carry-forward entails a negative interest effect as well as a negative cash flow effect, both of which reduce the profitability of an investment. If a foreign loss is accounted for in the residence country and investors are in an overall profit situation, an immediate loss deduction is available. If the foreign loss is excluded from domestic income, e.g. because the loss is suffered by a tax exempt foreign permanent establishment, the loss may only be carried forward in the foreign country. In this case, investors who expect losses, e.g. initial losses, will prefer foreign countries which do not restrict the loss carry forward. The same is true for losses suffered by foreign subsidiaries, because these losses are trapped in the foreign subsidiary.

3.2.6. Transfer Pricing

3.2.6.1. Subsidiary

Multinational groups have an incentive to shift taxable profits to low-taxed subsidiaries via transfer pricing. Given the lack of comparable market transactions, transfer prices in most cases are far from being precise. Consequently, transfer price tax planning enjoys considerable room for maneuver. Multinational groups may manipulate transfer prices in order to reduce the groups' overall tax burden.

Investment location decisions and profit shifting through transfer prices are interrelated. A corporation may invest in a high tax country through a subsidiary if it is able to shift the profits out of the high-tax country to a low-taxed subsidiary. This means that the profits earned in the high-taxed country are subject to a low tax rate. Profit shifting then increases the investment's NPV in the high-tax country and may decouple the investment decision from the tax rate.

Statutory Tax Rate

International tax planning through transfer pricing is driven by the statutory tax rate. One euro of shifted profit saves an amount of taxes that is determined by the difference between the statutory profit tax rates of the two corporations involved in profit shifting. The more profit is shifted to a low-taxed foreign subsidiary, the more the overall tax burden approaches the foreign corporation tax rate.

Example (3.8): G Corporation, resident in country G, delivers 1,000 units of goods (production cost of 90) to the affiliated S Corporation, resident in country S, at a stipulated price (transfer price) of 100 per unit. S Corporation sells the good to a third party at a price of 130 per unit. The pre-tax profit per unit amounts to 130 – 90 = 40, which translates in an overall pre-tax profit of 40.000. G Corporation and S Corporation are subject to corporation tax at a rate of 30% and 20% respectively. Three cases are compared. (i) Both countries consider the transfer price of 100 to be at arm's length. (ii) Both countries consider the transfer price of 100 not be at arm's length and adjust it to 125. (iii) Country G adjusts the transfer price to 125, whereas country S assumes the transfer price of 100 to be at arm's length.

			Case 1	Case 2	Case 3
	Country G		Price: 100	Price: 125	Price: 125
1	Profit before taxes		10,000	35,000	35,000
2	Corporation tax	30% · (1)	3,000	10,500	10,500
	Country S		Price: 100	Price: 125	Price: 100
3	Profit before tax		30,000	5,000	30,000
4	Corporation tax	20% · (3)	6,000	1,000	6,000
	Overall tax position				
5	Pre-tax profit		40,000	40,000	40,000
6	Overall taxes	(2) + (4)	9,000	11,500	16,500
7	After-tax profit	(5) - (6)	31,000	28,500	23,500
8	Tax burden (%)	(6) / (5)	22.50	28.75	41.25

In case (1), 75% of overall profit (30,000 of 40,000) is allocated to the low-tax country S. The overall tax burden is therefore close to the corporation tax rate of country S. In case (2), 87.5% of overall profit (35,000 of 40,000) is allocated to country G. The overall tax burden is close to the corporation tax rate in country G. In case (3), the tax bases overlap. Profit of 25,000 is allocated to both countries and the aggregated tax base amounts to 65,000. Double taxation arises and the overall tax burden is above the corporation tax rate in country G.

Aggressive transfer pricing may not only result in double taxation due to overlapping tax bases. In addition, costs to comply with the law may increase, given the strict documentation requirements imposed on corporations.

Restrictions

Tax law tackles prices stipulated in contracts concluded by corporations and shareholders which are not at arm's length. German corporation tax law, for example, deals with hidden profit distributions to the shareholders as well as with hidden capital contributions to the corporations.[16] A hidden profit distribution occurs if, in a deal, the payment of a German subsidiary to its foreign parent (the shareholder) is higher than in a comparable situation between independent parties. For tax purposes, the amount paid in excess the arm's length price is added back to the corporate income of the German subsidiary. A hidden capital contribution occurs if, in a deal, a German parent (the shareholder) receives a payment lower than the third party price in a comparable situation. For tax purposes the taxable income of the parent is increased and the difference is added to the book value of its shareholding in the foreign subsidiary.

According to German tax law, benefits granted to a corporation by shareholders, which cannot be regarded as an asset, do not qualify as hidden capital contribution. Sec. 1 of the Foreign Tax Act (AStG) closes the loophole which otherwise would exist. Transfer prices of such benefits have to be adjusted other tax rules notwithstanding, if the taxable income of German taxpayers was reduced by pricing the transaction at other than arm´s length.

Frictions

Transfer prices simulate market co-ordination within a decentralized organization[17] and affect the profit allocation to decentralized business units. In practice, transfer prices are the result of a compromise between different functions of transfer pricing, namely, internal co-ordination and internal profit allocation.[18] Tax planning adds another function to transfer pricing leading to costs in terms of tax-induced distortions of internal co-ordination and profit allocation. As a result, companies may use two separate sets of transfer prices. However, two sets of

---

[16] See Sec. 8 (3) Corporation Tax Act (KStG).

[17] See Schmalenbach (1947) and Hirshleifer (1956).

[18] See Ewert and Wagenhofer (2008) pp. 579-580.

transfer prices may adversely affect the acceptance of the company´s transfer price system within the company.

Additional costs arise from documentation obligations. Companies are obliged by tax law to report the methods and data used in intra-group transactions. Tax compliance costs increase in frequency and in complexity of intra-group transactions.[19]

3.2.6.2. Permanent Establishment

Under the authorized OECD approach, the permanent establishment is treated as a functionally separate and independent enterprise. The profit of a foreign permanent establishment is determined on the basis of a functional analysis which identifies functions performed, assets owned or used and risks assumed. The dealings between the principal company and the permanent establishment are determined by assessing transfer prices which are used in case of legally separated entities (i.e. corporations). Thus the multinational company has again some room for maneuver.

Exemption Method

The economic effects of shifting profit to a foreign permanent establishment depend on the method of avoiding double taxation. If the principal company's country of residence applies the exemption method, the tax burden in the (foreign) source country is final. The more profit is taxed in the source country, the closer the overall tax burden comes to that country´s corporation tax rate. Conversely, the more profit is taxed in the residence country, the closer the overall tax burden comes to the residence country's corporation tax.

Example (3.9): G Corporation is resident in country G and delivers 1,000 units of goods (production cost of 95) to a permanent establishment in country S at a transfer price of 100 per unit. The permanent establishment sells the good to a third party at a price of 125 per unit. The pre-tax profit per unit amounts to 125 – 95 = 30, which translates in an overall pre-tax profit of 30,000. G Corporation is subject to corporation tax at a rate of 30%. The permanent establishment's profits are taxed at a rate of 20% in country S (limited tax liability). Three cases are compared. (i) Both countries consider the transfer price of 100 to be at arm's length. (ii) Both countries consider the transfer price of 100 not to be at arm's length and adjust it to 120. (iii) Country G adjusts the transfer price to 120, whereas country S assumes the transfer price of 100 to be at arm's length. Country G exempts profits generated by foreign permanent establishments.

---

[19] A survey among European companies suggests that transfer pricing documentations are associated with a rise in tax compliance costs of about 135% to 178%. See European Communities (2004), pp. 41.

Exemption Method					
			Case 1	Case 2	Case 3
	Country G		Price: 100	Price: 120	Price: 120
1	Profit before taxes		5,000	25,000	25,000
2	Corporation tax	30% · (1)	1,500	7,500	7,500
	Country S		Price: 100	Price: 120	Price: 100
3	Profit before taxes		25,000	5,000	25,000
4	Corporation tax	20% · (3)	5,000	1,000	5,000
	Overall tax position				
5	Pre-tax profit		30,000	30,000	30,000
6	Overall taxes	(2) + (4)	6,500	8,500	12,500
7	After-tax profit	(5) - (6)	23,500	21,500	17,500
8	Tax burden (%)	(6) / (5)	21.67	28.33	41.67

The tax burden in case (1) approaches the statutory income tax rate in country S, indicating that G Corporation has successfully shifted profit to the low-tax country S. The tax burden in case (3) exceeds the statutory tax rate in country G, indicating legal double taxation of profits.

The exemption method provides corporations with a strong incentive to shift profits to low-taxed foreign permanent establishments. In case of foreign losses the tax incentive is reverse. A high-taxed corporation has an incentive to shift losses from low-tax countries to the domestic tax base where the losses are deducted from high-taxed profits.

Credit Method

If the principal company's country of residence applies the credit method, the country of residence includes foreign profits in the taxable income of the principal company. The foreign profits are taxed at the rate of the parent company. Foreign income tax is credited against the income tax of the parent company.

Example (3.10): The assumptions of Example (3.9) apply. Country G taxes the worldwide income and grants a foreign tax credit.

Credit Method					
			(1)	(2)	(3)
	Country G		Price: 100	Price: 120	Price: 120
1	Profit before taxes		30,000	30,000	30,000
2	Corporation tax	30% · (1)	9,000	9,000	9,000
3	Foreign tax credit		5,000	1,000	1,000
4	Income taxes paid	(2) – (3)	4,000	8,000	8,000
	Country S		Price: 100	Price: 120	Price: 100
5	Profit before taxes		25,000	5,000	25,000
6	Corporation tax	20% · (3)	5,000	1,000	5,000
	Overall tax position				
7	Pre-tax profit		30,000	30,000	30,000
8	Overall taxes	(4) + (6)	9,000	9,000	13,000
9	After-tax profit	(7) - (8)	21,000	21,000	17,000
10	Tax burden (%)	(8) / (7)	30.00	30.00	43.33

In case (1) and (2), the total tax burden is determined by the statutory corporation tax rate of country G. In case (3), the foreign corporation tax credit is limited to the amount of domestic corporation taxes on the foreign profit determined according to the rules applicable in country G. From country G's perspective, the foreign profit amounts to 5,000 (= 125,000 – 120,000), which leads to creditable foreign income taxes of the amount of 1,000 (= 20% · 5,000). As a result of the overlapping tax bases, G Corporation suffers from double taxation and the overall tax burden is higher than the corporation tax rate in country G.

Under the credit method, the principal company does not have an incentive to shift profits to a low-tax country. The international allocation of profits does not influence the overall tax burden as long as both countries agree on the arm's length transfer price. Then, only the tax rate of the principal company matters. Yet, in case of conflicting transfer price assessments and an excess credit situation double taxation of foreign profits is unavoidable.

Restrictions

Internal dealings do not affect the tax base of a company because there is no legal contract between the domestic company and its foreign permanent establishment. As opposed to dealings with foreign subsidiaries, dealings with foreign permanent establishments cannot be subject to restrictions which are targeted at prices stipulated in legal contracts.

Nevertheless, the profits attributed to a foreign permanent establishment have to conform to the arm's length principle. According to the OECD-MT, the profits that are attributable to the permanent establishment are the profits it might be expected to make, in particular in its dealings with the principal company, if it were a separate and independent enterprise engaged in the same or similar activities under the same or similar conditions, Art. 7 (2). National tax law usually applies the same principles.

3.2.7. Outbound Transfer of Assets

Profits may be shifted by means of asset transfers, e.g. by transferring an asset from a domestic business to a foreign corporation. From a pure tax perspective, the investor faces the choice between realizing the asset's hidden reserves in the home country or transferring it to a foreign country for hidden reserve realization there. If the pre-tax cash flows are the same in both countries, investors choose the location where the NPV of tax payments is lower.

Yet, the transfer of hidden reserves has additional effects. The home country where the hidden reserves accrued may tax them (exit taxation) and the foreign country to which they are transferred may allow their deduction as business expenses (e.g. as depreciation) by providing a step-up in the asset´s value. Both effects impact on the NPV of taxes in the opposite direction. The exit of the asset triggers a tax payment and the entry of the asset may result in tax savings. The tax payments and tax savings depend on the tax rates of the respective country (tax rate effect). If the tax payments in the home country and the tax savings in the foreign country are spread over time, the NPV of the tax payments and the NPV of the tax savings depends on the interest rate (timing effect).

Investors purchasing a depreciable asset at time $t = 0$ and expecting risk-free cash flows CF_t determine the after-tax NPV $C_0^{\tau,H} > 0$ if the profitable investment is carried out in the investors' country of residence. If investors transfer the asset immediately after purchase to a foreign country where the investment is carried out, the after-tax NPV amounts to $C_0^{\tau,F} > 0$. In the latter case, investors additionally have to take into account the exit tax upon the transfer of the asset and the tax savings upon entry into the foreign country.

Given the tax book value BV_0 and the market value MV_0 of the asset respectively, the hidden reserve at time $t = 0$ amounts to $HR_0 = MV_0 - BV_0$. The hidden reserve is transferred at time $t = 0$ and the asset is recognized in the tax balance sheet of the foreign country at market value MV_0. The total tax effect of the asset transfer in present value terms then amounts to

(3.19) $$TET_0 = HR_0 \cdot [-\tau_H \cdot \alpha_H \cdot R_H(i_\tau, n_H) + \tau_F \cdot \alpha_F \cdot R_F(i_\tau, n_F)]$$

where τ_H and τ_F denote the statutory profit tax rates of the home country H and the foreign country F respectively. $R_*(i_\tau, n_*)$ represents the annuity factor.[20] The tax upon exit of the asset may be paid immediately ($\alpha_H = 1, R_H = 1$) or may be deferred over n_H periods ($n_H > 1, \alpha_H = \frac{1}{n_H}$). In the foreign country, the asset may be immediately expensed ($\alpha_F = 1, R_F = 1$) or depreciated on a straight-line basis over n_F periods ($n_F > 1, \alpha_F = \frac{1}{n_F}$).

The first term in the brackets of equation (3.19) indicates the present value of the home country's tax on the hidden reserves upon transfer of the asset, taking into account the possible deferral of exit taxes; the second term denotes the present value of the tax savings in the foreign country due to depreciation of the hidden reserves transferred. The investor prefers a transfer of the asset to the foreign country if

(3.20) $$C_0^{\tau,F} + TET_0 > C_0^{\tau,H}.$$

Condition (3.20) indicates a tax advantage of the foreign investment if the after-tax NPV of the investment in country F, taking into account the tax effect of the asset transfer, exceeds the after-tax NPV of the investment in country H.

Lock-In Effect and Lock-Out Effect

If the tax base (CF_t - D_t) and the tax rates are the same in both countries ($\tau_H = \tau_F = \tau$), investors are able to transfer the asset to the foreign country without changing the NPV ($C_0^{\tau,H} = C_0^{\tau,F}$). Yet, the exit taxation is the decisive factor. A lock-in effect, impeding the asset transfer, occurs if exit taxes are not deferred ($\alpha_H = 1, R_H = 1$) and if the tax savings in the foreign country are spread over time ($n_F > 1, \alpha_F = \frac{1}{n_F}$). Then $TET_0 = -\tau \cdot HR_0 \cdot \left[1 - \frac{1}{n_F} \cdot R(i_\tau, n_F)\right] < 0$ and the above condition (3.20) is not true. Yet, given a tax rate differential, the transfer of the asset may be tax-advantageous, i.e. a lock out-effect may also occur.

Example (3.11): H Corporation, located in country H, acquires a depreciable asset at time t = 0 at the price of 100; the asset's hidden reserve amounts to HR_0 = 10. H Corporation considers transferring the asset at t = 0 to a subsidiary located in country F. The corporation tax rates amount to τ_H = 30% and τ_F = 20% respectively. In both countries, the asset is depreciated straight line over n = 2 years. H corporation discounts the cash flows at the net interest rate $i_\tau = 7\%$; the annuity factor amounts to $R(7\%, 2) = 1.81$. H Corporation compares the after-tax NPVs of the investment in country H and F.

---

20 The annuity factor amounts to $R_*(i_\tau, n_*) = \frac{1}{i_\tau} \cdot \left[1 - \frac{1}{(1+i_\tau)^{n_*}}\right]$ where i_τ designates the investor's after-tax market interest rate.

t	0	1	2
Country H			
I_0	-100.00		
CF_t		60.50	66.55
D_t		50.00	50.00
$T_t = \tau_H \cdot (CF_t - D_t)$		3.15	4.97
$I_0 + CF_t - T_t$	-100.00	57.35	61.59
NPV after taxes	$C_0^{\tau,H} = -100 + \frac{60.5 - 3.15}{1.07} + \frac{66.55 - 4.97}{1.07^2} = 7.39$		
Country F			
I_0	-100.00		
CF_t		60.50	66.55
D_t		50.00	50.00
$T_t = \tau_F \cdot (CF_t - D_t)$		2.10	3.31
$I_0 + CF_t - T_t$	-100.00	58.40	63.24
NPV after taxes	$C_0^{\tau,F} = -100 + \frac{60.5 - 2.1}{1.07} + \frac{66.55 - 3.31}{1.07^2} = 9.82$		

H Corporation experiences a tax incentive to transfer the asset to country F because the transfer increases the investment's after-tax NPV by 2.43 (= 9.82 – 7.39). However, upon transfer, H Corporation has to pay corporation tax on the asset's hidden reserve $HR_0 = 10$ in the amount of 3 $(=30\% \cdot 10)$. If country F takes up the asset for tax purposes at the value of $MV_0 = 110$ (acquisition cost of 100 plus hidden reserve of 10), the tax savings due to the additional depreciation of 10 amount to 1.81 $\left(=20\% \cdot \frac{1}{2} \cdot 10 \cdot 1.81\right)$. The total tax effect TET_0 of the asset transfer according to equation (3.19) is negative and amounts to -1.19 $(=-3+1.81)$. Nevertheless, H Corporation will transfer the asset, because according to equation (3.20) $9.82 - 1.19 > 7.39$. On balance, the asset transfer increases the investment's after-tax NPV by 1.24 (= 9.82 – 1.19 – 7.39). H Corporation experiences a lock-out effect.

Tax Deferral

German income tax law, as does the income tax law of many other countries, prescribes immediate taxation of hidden reserves upon outbound transfer of assets. A tax deferral is only provided for fixed assets which are transferred to a permanent establishment located in an EU Member State. Technically, the taxation is deferred by carry-forward of the difference between the asset's market value and its book value as deferred income.[21] The deferred income is taken up in the year of transfer and released over the following five years.

Example (3.12): A Corporation located in Germany transfers an asset to its permanent establishment in France. The asset's acquisition cost amounts to 200 and the market value is 300. In the year of the transfer, A Corporation takes up deferred income of 100 in its tax computations. In the following five years, the deferred income is reduced by 20 per year. As a result, the taxable profit increases by 20 each year and the hidden reserve of 100 is fully taxed. A Corporation takes advantage of both positive cash flow effects and interest effects.

In respect of cross-border transactions covered by the MD, Germany exercises its taxing right as prescribed therein. If a German corporation transfers its tax residence to another country, Germany prescribes exit taxation on the basis of the market value of the assets wherever Germany's taxing right would be excluded or restricted by the transfer.[22] The same is true in case of cross-border mergers. Tax deferral, as provided for asset transfers to a foreign permanent establishment, is not available upon outbound transfer of seat or merger onto a foreign entity. The hidden reserves of assets belonging to a German permanent establishment are taxed immediately if non-EU countries are involved, i.e. if the transaction is not covered by the MD.

3.3. Financing Decisions

3.3.1. Internal Debt

The parent company may contribute equity capital to the foreign subsidiary (new equity financing). Alternatively, the investment of the foreign subsidiary may be financed with a loan granted by the parent company (internal debt). From a tax perspective, the choice between equity and debt has far reaching consequences.

---

[21] See Sec. 4g German Income Tax Act (EStG).

[22] See Sec. 12 German Corporation Tax Act (KStG).

Tax Asymmetries

The cost of debt capital is tax-deductible. The tax law follows civil law which obliges the debtor to pay interest on the loan and grants the creditor a claim to the interest payments. The cost of equity capital, on the other hand, is not tax-deductible. Again tax law follows civil law, which grants the owner of equity capital a residual claim to the net cash flows. In the international tax arena, profits are in principle taxed where they are generated (source principle) whereas interest income is taxed where the recipient of interest payments is resident (residence principle). As a result, the choice between equity and internal debt entails the choice of where to be taxed on the capital income.

Economic Effects

In the case of equity financing, the foreign subsidiary earns profits which are burdened with foreign corporation tax because the subsidiary is subject to unlimited tax liability. Distributed profits may be subject to foreign withholding taxes. Dividends received by the domestic parent company are usually tax-free if the parent company is a corporation. Profits distributed by the corporate parent to natural persons (as ultimate shareholders) are usually taxed under a shareholder relief system. As a result, the tax burden of equity financed investments is determined by foreign profit taxes and both foreign and domestic taxes upon the distribution of profits.

In the case of debt financing, interest payments on loans are tax-deductible by the foreign corporation and the corresponding interest income is taxed when received by the domestic company granting the (internal) loan. The foreign country may levy a withholding tax on interest payments (limited tax liability of the creditor). Within the EU, the Interest and Royalties Directive prevents Member States from levying withholding taxes. Withholding taxes are creditable against corporation tax on the interest income received if a corporation grants the loan. If there are no restrictions on interest deductibility and provided any withholding taxes are fully credited, the tax burden is exclusively determined by the corporation tax of the corporation granting the internal loan.

Tax Shield

Debt financing generates a tax shield because tax-deductible interest payments reduce corporation tax. If interest payments of the amount $I = r \cdot L_t$ of a corporation to its shareholders permanently substitute the same amount of profit, the tax shield is determined by dividend tax rate τ_D and the interest income tax rate τ_I as well as the corporation tax rate τ_C. The interest tax shield amounts to

$$TS = \frac{r \cdot L \cdot [\tau_D - \tau_I + (1-\tau_D) \cdot \tau_C]}{i_\tau} \quad (3.21)$$

where i_τ denotes the after-tax market interest rate. The first and the second term in the brackets of equation (3.21) denote the income tax rate effect of switching from equity to debt; the third term in the brackets indicates the corporation tax savings taking into account dividend taxation. If dividends and interest income are taxed at the same rate ($\tau_D = \tau_I$) and the tax payments are discounted at the market interest rate ($i_\tau = r$), the tax shield reduces to $TS = L \cdot (1 - \tau_D) \cdot \tau_C$ and indicates the corporation tax savings after dividend taxes.

The interest tax shield created by an internal loan which is granted by a domestic corporate parent to a foreign subsidiary (ignoring the shareholders of the corporate parent and assuming tax exemption of inter-corporate dividends) can be derived by setting $\tau_D = 0$, $\tau_I = \tau_{CH}$, $\tau_C = \tau_{CF}$ and by discounting with the market interest rate r:

(3.22) $$TS = L \cdot (-\tau_{CH} + \tau_{CF}).$$

Equation (3.22) denotes the interest tax shield from the perspective of a domestic corporate parent which receives inter-corporate dividends tax-free and which is fully taxed on interest income at the tax rate τ_{CH}. Under these conditions, it is tax efficient for the domestic parent to finance a foreign subsidiary with internal debt if the subsidiary is located in a high tax country ($\tau_{CH} < \tau_{CF}$). Conversely, if the foreign subsidiary's tax rate is lower than the parent's tax rate ($\tau_{CH} > \tau_{CS}$) the tax shield is negative and the parent will prefer equity financing to debt financing.

Example (3.13): H Corporation, resident in country H, wholly owns F Corporation, a subsidiary located in country F. H Corporation is considering an investment of 100 perpetually yielding a pre-tax return of 20%. H Corporation evaluates whether to finance the investment in country F with new equity or with an internal loan at 10%. The corporation tax rates of H Corporation and of F Corporation amount to 10% and 30% respectively. Withholding tax is not levied upon the distribution of F Corporation's profits. H Corporation receives dividends tax-free. The after-tax market interest rate amounts to 10%.

			New Equity		Debt	
	t		0	$1-\infty$	0	$1-\infty$
	F Corporation					
1	EBIT	20%·100	-	20.00	-	20.00
2	Interest payments	10%·100	-	-	-	10.00
3	Profit before taxes	(1)-(2)	-	20.00	-	10.00
4	Corporation tax	30%·(3)	-	6.00	-	3.00
5	Profit distribution	(3)-(4)	-	14.00	-	7.00

	G Corporation					
6	Interest income	(2)	-	-	-	10.00
7	Dividends	(5)	-	14.00	-	7.00
8	Corporation tax	10%·(6)	-	-	-	- 1.00
9	After-tax profit	(6)+(7)-(8)	-	14.00	-	16.00
10	Capital contribution		-100.00		-100.00	
11	Net cash flow	(9)+(10)	-100.00	14.00	-100.00	16.00
12	NPV		40.00		60.00	

Debt financing is preferable to equity financing because the profit tax rate (30%) is higher than the tax rate on interest income (10%). According to equation (3.22), the interest tax shield amounts to $TS = 100 \cdot (-10\% + 30\%) = 20$ indicating that debt financing is tax-advantaged. Accordingly, the difference in after-tax NPV amounts to 60.00 – 40.00 = 20.00.

Subsidiaries located in high-tax countries prefer debt financing. Foreign investors often seek to avoid equity financing of high-taxed subsidiaries, relying instead on internal loans granted by a low-taxed company. The interest tax shield in Germany, for instance, is determined by the corporation tax rate of 15%, the solidarity surcharge of 5.5% and the trade tax rate. For trade tax purposes only 75% of the interest payments are tax-deductible expenses. Assuming a trade tax rate of 14%, the relevant German tax rate amounts to 26.33% (= 15.83% + 75% · 14%) and may well exceed the corporation tax rate of foreign corporations providing loans to German subsidiaries.

Thin Capitalization Rules

A controlling foreign shareholder might increase the debt-equity ratio of a domestic subsidiary with an internal loan to reduce corporation taxes on profits earned by the subsidiary. Because of the tax incentive for debt financing, many countries have introduced thin capitalization (TC) rules. TC rules are designed to combat profit shifting through debt financing. Internal loans are less attractive if interest payments of the subsidiary receiving the loan are fully or partly non-deductible expenses.

As an example, the German TC rule restricts interest deductibility to 30% of the corporation's EBITDA (interest stripping rule).[23] Non-deductible interest expenses can be deducted in subsequent years subject to the restrictions on interest deductibility (interest carry forward). The interest carry-forward ensures that non-

[23] See Section 4h German Income Tax Act (EStG).

deductible interest expenses are not ultimately lost. If in subsequent years the earnings (EBITDA) increase or the debt- equity ratio decreases, the interest carry-forward results in deductible interest expenses. However, taxpayers suffer from a negative timing effect.

Example (3.14): Consider again example (3.13) and assume that F Corporation faces a TC rule of the German type. In this case, interest expenses are tax-deductible up to 30% of the EBITDA. Ignoring depreciation and amortization, tax-deductible interest expenses amount to 6 (=30% · 20) resulting in a taxable profit of 14 (= 20 – 6) and corporation tax of 4.20 (= 30% · 14). F Corporation's profit distribution is reduced to 5.80. If the interest income of H Corporation is fully taxed, H Corporation's profit distribution is reduced to 14.80 (= 10 + 5.80 – 1.00) which translates to an NPV of the debt financed investment of 48. The reduction in NPV by 12 reflects the increase in F Corporations income tax of 1.20 (= 4.20 – 3.00). Nevertheless H Corporation will still prefer debt financing to equity financing.

Note that the amount of interest payments not immediately tax-deductible has to be carried forward to subsequent years (interest carry-forward). Under the assumptions of example (3.13) F Corporation's actual interest expenses of 10 always exceed the tax deductible amount of 6. As a result, the interest carry-forward increases over time but can never be used by F Corporation.

The German interest stripping rule applies to all businesses subject to three conditions: (i) interest expenses exceeding interest income exceed a three million euro threshold, (ii) the business belongs to a group, and (iii) the leverage of a group company is higher than the group's total leverage. The interest stripping rule is therefore targeted at large resident companies which are higher leveraged than the international group to which they belong. The German rules are designed to protect small and medium sized businesses as well as independent companies.

3.3.2. External Debt

In many countries, among them Germany, interest expenses related to foreign investments may be tax-deductible, even though the profits they generate are not taxed. More specifically, domestic corporations may take up a loan and transfer the proceeds of the loan as an equity contribution to a foreign subsidiary. Interest expenses are tax-deductible, whereas profits of a foreign subsidiary are not taxed until distributed. Even then, the distribution is tax-free in the hands of a domestic corporation.

Tax Arbitrage

The asymmetric taxation of interest expenses and profit distributions offers strong incentives for corporations to engage in international tax rate arbitrage. By refinancing equity contributions to low-taxed foreign subsidiaries with external debt, interest payments of a multinational group can save taxes in a high-tax country, although profits related to the respective capital are taxed in low-tax countries.

Consider a domestic corporation taking up a loan at the market interest rate r and investing the proceeds in an equity contribution to a foreign subsidiary. This subsidiary invests the capital at a pre-tax rate of return of p. In case of a marginal investment the pre-tax net return amounts to zero. Taking taxes into account, the tax savings related to interest expenses deducted by the domestic corporation amount to τ_{CH}. The foreign subsidiary is taxed at the corporation tax rate τ_{CF}. The investment's after-tax return amounts to

$$(3.23) \qquad p \cdot (1 - \tau_{CF}) - r \cdot (1 - \tau_{CH}).$$

There is an opportunity for tax rate arbitrage, if the foreign corporation tax rate is lower than the domestic corporation rate ($\tau_{CF} < \tau_{CH}$). The tax advantage of a marginal investment ($p = r$) amounts to

$$(3.24) \qquad p \cdot (\tau_{CH} - \tau_{CF}) > 0.$$

Under these conditions, a German corporation can generate tax savings on investments with a pre-tax profit of zero.

Thin Capitalization Rules

TC rules are usually targeted at internal debt (debt financing by shareholders) and are thus not suitable for the prevention of international tax arbitrage through external debt. However, the tax rate arbitrage opportunities with respect to external debt have prompted some countries to extend their TC rules to cover external debt as well. The German TC rules, for example, apply to all kinds of debt financing. If the TC rule is applied, interest payments are not tax-deductible and do not immediately generate tax savings. The corporation taking out external debt to finance equity contributions to foreign corporations may pay taxes on a pre-tax profit of zero.

Example (3.15): A German parent corporation establishes a wholly owned subsidiary in country F with an equity contribution of 100. The subsidiary yields a perpetual profit of 10. The German corporation takes up a loan of 100 at an interest rate of 10% to refinance the equity contribution. The German parent corporation has sufficient profits to absorb the interest expenses. The corporation tax in country F amounts to 10%. The German trade tax rate amounts to 14% and the German corporation tax rate amounts to 15.83% (including solidarity surcharge) respectively. Upon profit distribution, the German parent has to pay taxes on 5% of the dividends received. Withholding taxes are not levied by Country F. Figures are rounded.

			No Restriction		Restriction	
	t		0	$1-\infty$	0	$1-\infty$
	F Corporation					
1	EBIT	10%·100	-	10.00	-	10.00
2	Corporation tax	10 %·(1)	-	-1.00	-	-1.00
3	Profit distribution	(1)+(2)	-	9.00	-	9.00
	G Corporation					
4	Interest payments	10%·100	-	- 10.00	-	-10.00
5	Dividends	(3)	-	9.00	-	9.00
6	Deductible interest			-10.00		0.00
7	Corporate income	(6)+5%·(5)	-	-9.55	-	0.45
8	Trade income	(7)-25%·(6)	-	-7.05	-	0.45
9	Corporation tax	15.83%·(7)	-	1.51	-	-0.07
10	Trade tax	14%·(8)	-	0.99	-	-0.06
11	Capital contribution		0.00	-	0.00	-
12	Net cash flow	(4)+(5) +(9)+(10)	-	1.50	-	-1.13
13	NPV		15.00		-11.30	

If G Corporation does not face a restriction on interest deductibility, it saves taxes at a rate of $\tau_{CH} = 15.83\% + 75\% \cdot 14\% = 26.33\%$ if the trade tax rate is 14%. Profits of the foreign subsidiary are taxed at τ_{CF}=10% and trigger additional German taxes when distributed to G Corporation. The German profit tax rate amounts to 29.83% (=15.83% + 14%) and is applied to 90% of the pre-tax profits distributed which translates in an additional profit tax burden of 1.34% (= 90% · 5% · 29.83%). The overall profit tax rate amounts to $\tau_{CF} = 10\% + 1.34\% = 11.34\%$. According to equation (3.24) the investments tax advantage is $10\% \cdot (26.33\% - 11.34\%) = 1.50\%$. In case G Corporation faces a restriction on interest deductibility ($\tau_{CH} = 0$), profits are still taxed at $\tau_{CF} = 11.34\%$. According to equation (3.24) the investment´s tax-disadvantage is $10\% \cdot (0\% - 11.34\%) = -1.13\%$.

When TC rules affect external debt financing, the corporations facing the restriction on debt have an incentive to transfer external debt to companies resident in countries where there are no comparable restrictions on the tax deductibility of interest payments. From a fiscal perspective, the TC rules are effective if domestic companies allocate external debt to foreign companies. In the above example (3.15), the German parent reduces the German corporation tax to zero if the loan is taken up by the foreign subsidiary. The foreign subsidiary's profit is reduced by the interest expenses and, as a result, the foreign corporation tax is also reduced to zero. The debt financed marginal investment is tax-free overall. In this case, taxes neither favor nor disadvantage equity financed investments which are refinanced with debt.

3.3.3. Profit Repatriation

Retained profits of a foreign subsidiary are not taxed until shareholders received them. Shareholders are therefore able to defer income taxes on foreign profits. The longer profits are retained by a foreign corporation, the less pronounced is the income tax burden on dividend distributions in present value terms. Thus, dividend taxes appear to matter.

The Irrelevance of Dividend Taxation

However, the decision to retain foreign profits does not depend on shareholders' dividend tax. It is the foreign corporation tax rate which matters. From a tax perspective, profits are to be retained if the foreign after-tax rate of return exceeds the domestic after-tax rate of return. More formally, given a foreign profit which can be distributed as dividend DIV either at $t = 0$ or at $t = n$, the tax advantage of profit retention is the difference in cash flow ΔCF_n at $t = n$ when comparing the distribution of the dividend at $t = 0$ with the distribution at $t = n$:

(3.25) $$\Delta CF_n = DIV \cdot (1 - \tau_D) \cdot \left[\left(1 + i_{\tau,CF}\right)^n - (1 + i_\tau)^n\right].$$

The variable τ_D denotes the income tax rate on dividends. The variable $i_{\tau,CF}$ and i_τ indicate the foreign corporation's after-tax rate of return and the domestic shareholders' after-tax rate of return of a capital market investment respectively. Income taxes on dividends affect the amount of cash flow available to shareholders. However, these taxes do not influence the decision to repatriate the foreign profit.

After-tax Rate of Return

Shareholders do not repatriate the foreign profit if the foreign after-tax rate of return exceeds the domestic after-tax rate of return ($i_{\tau,CF} > i_\tau$). Given a uniform pre-tax rate of return, the foreign corporation tax rate and the domestic income tax rate on interest income are decisive.

Example (3.16): G Corporation holds 100% of the shares of foreign F Corporation. F Corporation has retained profits of 100 which can be reinvested at the pre-tax rate of return of 10%. The foreign corporation tax rate is 10%. G Corporation's profits tax rate is 30%; dividends received are taxed at 1.5%. At time $t = 3$, G Corporation compares the cash flow of repatriation at time $t = 3$ and at time $t = 0$. G Corporation's shareholders are neglected. If G Corporation repatriates the foreign profits at t = 0, corporate tax on dividends is paid at t = 0. The after-tax profit distribution is invested at the after-tax market interest rate of 7%.

	t		0	1	2	3
1	Dividend		100.00			
2	Dividend tax	1.5% · (1)	1.50			
3	Capital market investment		98.50	105.39	112.77	0.00
4	Interest income			9.85	10.54	11.28
5	Corporation tax	30% · (4)		2.96	3.16	3.38
6	Reinvestment			6.89	7.38	7.90
7	After-tax cash flow					120.67

Alternatively, G Corporation defers the repatriation of the foreign profits to time $t = 3$.

	t		0	1	2	3
1	Profit reserve		100.00	109.00	118.81	0.00
2	Pre-tax profits			10.00	10.90	11.88
3	Corporation tax	10% · (2)		1.00	1.09	1.19
4	After-tax profit	(2) – (3)		9.00	9.81	10.69
5	Profit distribution			0.00	0.00	129.50
6	Profit retention			9.00	9.81	0.00
7	Corporation tax	1.5% · (5)				1.94
8	After-tax cash flow	(5) – (7)				127.56

C Corporation's net rate of return is 9% (= 10% - 10% · 10%), whereas the after-tax rate of return of G Corporation's investments is 7% (=10% - 30% · 10%). As a result, the after-tax cash flow at time $t = 3$ on deferred profit distribution exceeds the after-tax cash flow at time $t = 3$ on immediate profit distribution by 6.89 (= 127.56 – 120.67), which is the additional cash flow determined by equation (3.25): $6.89 = 100 \cdot \left(1 - 1.5\%\right) \cdot \left[(1 + 9\%)^3 - (1 + 7\%)^3\right]$.

The shareholders' income taxes on profit distributions are irrelevant for the decision to repatriate the foreign profits. Shareholder taxation does not matter because the shareholders are unable to avoid income taxes on distributed foreign earnings.

CFC Legislation

Given the incentive to accumulate capital in foreign low-taxed corporations, the shareholder's country of residence will often implement Controlled Foreign Corporations (CFC) legislation. If CFC rules apply, the foreign corporate profit is included in the current income of the shareholders. The lower foreign corporation tax rate is no longer effective because the shareholders' domestic income tax rate applies to the foreign income. Subsequent profit distributions are usually tax-free insofar as the distributed profits have already been taxed when allocated to the shareholders.

Given the profit *DIV* of a foreign corporation at $t = 0$ which is reinvested at the market interest rate and distributed at $t = n$ to the corporate shareholder, subject to CFC legislation, the shareholder's net cash flow at $t = 3$ amounts to

$$CF_t = DIV \cdot (1 + i_\tau)^n - \tau_D \cdot DIV. \tag{3.26}$$

The first term of equation (3.26) indicates that foreign profits stemming from the profit reserve *DIV* are subject to tax at the shareholder level. If foreign taxes can be credited, which is assumed in equation (3.26), the after-tax return of the foreign capital market investment is determined by the shareholder´s income tax rate. Profits already burdened with shareholder taxes are tax-free for the shareholder when distributed. The distribution of the profit reserve *DIV*, which has not been subject to CFC legislation, triggers taxes at the shareholder level. Equation (3.26) makes clear that CFC rules remove the opportunity to accumulate capital at high net rates of return in a foreign company.

Example (3.17): The assumptions of Example (3.16) apply. Under the CFC rules of G Corporations residence country, F Corporation's profits derived from the reinvestment of retained earnings of 100 at the capital market are included in G Corporation's taxable income and taxed at a rate of 30%. Foreign corporation taxes are credited against the income tax liability of G Corporation. F Corporation distributes profits up to an amount necessary to cover the taxes of G Corporation.

	t		0	1	2	3
	F Corporation					
1	Profit reserve		100.00	107.00	114.49	0.00
2	Pre-tax profits			10.00	10.70	11.45
3	Corporation tax	10% · (2)		1.00	1.07	1.14
4	After-tax profit	(2) – (3)		9.00	9.63	10.30
5	Profit distribution			2.00	2.14	124.79
6	Profit retention			7.00	7.49	0.00
	G Corporation					
7	CFC income	(2)		10.00	10.70	11.45
8	Profit taxes	30% · (2)		3.00	3.21	4.93
9	Foreign tax credit	(3)		1.00	1.07	1.14
10	Taxes paid	(8) – (9)		2.00	2.14	3.79
11	After-tax cash flow					121.00

Total taxes paid on F Corporation's profit amount to 30% of pre-tax profits. Distributed profits subject to CFC rules are tax-free whereas the distribution of profits not subject to CFC rules is taxed at the dividend tax rate of 1.5%. G Corporation's profit tax at $t = 3$ (row 8) is calculated as $4.93 = 1.50\% \cdot 100 + 30\% \cdot 11.45$. Compared to the case where income taxes are deferred without any restriction - Example (3.16) - the cash flow at time $t = 3$ drops from 127.56 to 121.00, which is the cash flow determined by equation (3.26): $121.00 = 100 \cdot (1 + 7\%)^3 - 1{,}5\% \cdot 100$.

Foreign profits which are subject to CFC rules are currently included in the shareholder's taxable income and, thus, are not taxed under the dividend taxation scheme. Because the yield of the foreign investment is currently taxed as business income by the shareholder, CFC rules reduce the after-tax rate of return of the foreign investment to that of a domestic investment.

3.4. Special Purpose Entities

3.4.1. Finance Companies

The organizational structure of a multinational group influences the tax burden of the group's investments. Group companies may serve special purposes to improve the overall tax position of a multinational group. It is a common tax planning strategy to interpose finance companies in low tax countries in order to transform equity capital to debt and to make use of the tax asymmetries between equity and debt financing.

The typical structure of a finance company scheme is as follows: The finance company is located in a country with low tax rates or favorable tax rules for finance companies, such as in Belgium, Ireland, Luxembourg or the Netherlands. The finance company is funded with equity capital by the high-taxed parent company. The finance company forwards its equity capital to subsidiaries in high-tax countries by granting loans.

Economic Effects

Interposing a finance company enables earnings of foreign subsidiaries to be transferred as tax-deductible interest payments to the finance company where the corresponding interest income is subject to low corporation tax. Repatriation of the finance companies' profits to the ultimate parent company does not, as a rule, trigger additional taxes. In effect, foreign profits are taxed at the corporation tax rate that is applicable in the country where the finance company is resident.

Example (3.18): P Corporation, located in country P, is considering an investment in country S through a local subsidiary. P Corporation contributes equity capital of 1,000 to the foreign subsidiary. The investment in country S generates a pre-tax return of 5% on the equity capital invested which equals the capital market rate of return. The corporation tax rates in countries P and S are both 30% respectively. The subsidiary´s net profit in country S amounts to 35 (= 50 – 30% · 50) and can be tax-free distributed to P Corporation.

P Corporation is considering interposing a finance company in country B. The corporation tax rate in country B is 35%. However, there is a notional interest deduction of 4% on the equity capital of finance companies. P Corporation contributes equity capital of 1,000 to the finance company. The finance company forwards the capital to the subsidiary in country S as a loan at an interest rate of 5% resulting in an interest payment of 50. The subsidiary's pre-tax earnings of 50 are completely shifted to the finance company in country B through interest payments. A notional interest of 40 (= 4% · 1,000) is deducted from the finance company's interest income of 50, which reduces the finance company's tax base to 10 and results in a tax payment of 3.5 (= 35% · 10). Due to the notional interest deduction, the profit of the finance company is effectively taxed at 7% (= 3.5/50) and can be distributed tax-free to P Corporation. By interposing the finance company, P Corporation manages to reduce the tax burden from 30% to 7% which translates into a net profit of 46.5 (= 50 – 7% · 50).

The interposition of a finance company reduces the corporation tax revenue of the countries where the parent company and the subsidiary are resident. Firstly, the country where the debt financed subsidiary is resident suffers from a loss in corporation tax revenue from the tax-deductible interest expenses. Secondly, the country where the parent company is resident forgoes corporation tax revenue because taxable interest income is channeled through the finance company and thus transformed into tax-free dividend income. The country where the finance company is resident increases its tax revenue because it attracts finance companies.

Restrictions

The success of a tax planning strategy based on a low-taxed finance company depends on TC rules in the country where the debt financed subsidiary is located (source country) and on CFC rules in the country where the shareholder of the finance company is resident (residence country).

If the source country applies TC rules and restricts the deductibility of interest payments to the finance company, the group may face double taxation due to conflicting qualifications of interest payments. Income taxes are charged on the non-deductible amount of the interest payments (which are regarded as profits) in the source country. The finance company's country of residence levies income taxes on the interest payments (which are regarded as interest income).

If CFC rules apply in the shareholder's residence country, the shareholding parent company is taxed on the profits of the finance company at regular tax rates. The corporation taxes of the finance company may or may not be credited against the income taxes of the parent company. However, the source country's corporation taxes charged on the non-deductible amount of interest payments will not be creditable in the residence country, so the taxes due in the source country add to the taxes due in the residence country. Under these conditions, a tax planning strategy based on the interposition of a finance company may be unattractive.

Within the EU, some Member States exclude subsidiaries located in other EU Member States from the application of CFC rules and TC rules as well. If EU tax planning avoids TC rules and CFC rules, the finance company can use its low-taxed profits to grant new loans to high-taxed affiliates or distribute the low tax profits to the parent company. Because within the EU intra-group interest payments do not trigger withholding taxes, the finance company receives the interest income free of foreign taxes and avoids a possible excess credit situation. Withholding taxes are not levied on intra-group dividends of EU corporations. Thus, the corporate parent, as a rule, does not pay taxes on the dividends received from the finance company. If the repatriation of the finance company's profits is tax-free, the parent company is able to invest low taxed foreign profits at home or abroad.

3.4.2. Holding Companies

A parent company has the choice to either directly hold the shares of a foreign company or to interpose a foreign holding company, which in turn owns the shares of the foreign company. From a tax planning perspective, holding companies can be interposed to make use of foreign group taxation regimes. Because group taxation regimes are usually restricted to resident companies, the holding company and the affiliated companies have to be resident in the same country to form a group for tax purposes. To establish a tax group in the foreign country, the shareholdings in the foreign subsidiaries are transferred to a foreign holding company which in exchange issues new shares.

Example (3.19): G Corporation owns 100% of the shares of FP Corporation and FL Corporation both located in country F. G Corporation establishes FH Corporation as a holding company in country F to acquire the shares of FL Corporation and FP Corporation in exchange for its own shares. After the transaction is completed, G Corporation directly owns the shares of FH Corporation and, thus, indirectly owns the shares of FL Corporation and FP Corporation.

As a rule, the share exchange is tax-free. Capital gains on the exchange of shares are usually not taxed when earned by a corporation. Also, the tax rules on mergers usually exempt capital gains upon the exchange of controlling shareholdings from the tax base.

Loss Compensation Strategy

A foreign subsidiary is unable to transfer a loss to its parent company or to another affiliate. Most group taxation regimes are restricted to resident companies, thus excluding cross-border loss compensation. Holding companies enable the compensation of losses suffered by foreign subsidiaries. With the holding company, the parent company is in a position to consolidate a foreign subsidiary's losses with profits of other foreign subsidiaries resident in the same country.

Example (3.20): G Corporation owns 100% of the shares of FP Corporation and FL Corporation both located in country F. While FP Corporation earns profits in the amount of 500, FL Corporation suffers from a loss in the amount of 400 in the same year. Neither G Corporation nor FP Corporation is allowed to deduct FL Corporation's loss. Although FL Corporation may be allowed to carry forward the loss, the tax base in country F in the respective year amounts to 500, whereas the group´s profit in country F is only 100. If the foreign tax rate exceeds 20%, the group's tax burden is higher than the group's profit. G Corporation establishes the holding company FH Corporation. Under the group taxation rules of country F, FP Corporation, FL Corporation and FH Corporation form a tax group and reduce the group's taxable profit in country F to 100 (= 500 – 400).

Acquisition Strategy

Holding companies are not only used to offset losses immediately, but play also an important role when it comes to the acquisition of foreign companies with a share deal. The acquiring corporation will usually take up a loan to finance the acquisition price of the target company. After the acquisition, the target corporation may distribute its profits to finance the interest expenses of the acquiring corporation. Inter-corporate profit distributions are tax-free. As a result, the acquiring company may not be able to deduct the interest expenses from the distributed after-tax profits.

To achieve consolidation of the interest expenses with the profits of the target company, the acquiring corporation interposes a holding company. The holding company is granted a loan by the acquiring corporation and buys the shares in the target company. If the holding company and the target company are resident in the same country, the holding company can take advantage of a group taxation regime in the respective country. Once the group taxation regime applies, the profit of the target company is attributed to the holding company. As a result, the holding company is able to absorb the interest expenses with taxable profits of the target company.

Example (3.21): G Corporation located in country G considers the acquisition of F Corporation located in country F. F Corporation´s annual profit amounts to € 1,000,000. G Corporation establishes FH Corporation located in country F and subsequently grants a loan to FH Corporation to finance the acquisition of F Corporation. The annual interest expenses of FH Corporation are € 500,000 per year. FH Corporation acquires the shares of F Corporation and forms a group with F Corporation. F Corporation´s profit of € 1,000,000 is attributed to FH Corporation As a result, FH Corporation´s interest expenses are deducted from F Corporation's profit resulting in a taxable income of € 500,000.

Debt Strategy

Holding companies can also be used to accumulate debt in high-tax countries via internal share deals. In a first step, a corporation sells the shares in an affiliated corporation (the target company) located in a high-tax country to a locally resident holding company. This transaction takes place at the market value of the shares. As a rule, gains upon the sale of shares are tax-free for a corporation and so there is no immediate tax consequence. The holding company acquires the shares at a value above the book value of the selling corporation thus stepping up the shares' value. In a second step, the holding company takes up a loan in the amount of the book value of the newly acquired shares. The last step is for the holding company and the target company to form a tax group enabling the holding company to deduct the interest expenses from the taxable profits of the target company.

The holding company may take up either an internal loan or an external loan. If the loan is external, a multinational company increases the amount of debt allocated to the high tax country, establishing an interest tax shield. If the loan is internal, it is granted to the high-taxed holding company by a low-tax country finance company, ensuring that the corresponding interest income is low-taxed. As a result, the group manages to transfer taxable profits from a high-tax country through interest payments to a low-tax country. In both cases, the group successfully accumulates additional debt in a high-tax country without affecting the target company's leverage.

3.5. Empirical Evidence on International Tax Planning

There is much anecdotal evidence among tax professionals on how taxes influence multinational companies' decisions. Yet, anecdotal evidence does not provide reliable empirical information. Empirical tax research must be based on economic theory dealing with the economic effects of tax planning. Empirical tax research takes into account the premises and predictions of tax planning models and systematically investigates how taxes influence business decisions.

The main problem of empirical tax research based on historical data (e.g. financial accounting data) is to isolate the tax effect from other economic effects which may be responsible for the investors' behavior. If, for example, it is observed that in a certain country the corporations' debt-equity ratio increases with an increasing corporation tax rate, steps must be taken to rule out all possible non-tax reasons (e.g. the business cycle) for the corporations' increased indebtedness.

By contrast to a national setting, comparable companies in different countries are subject to different tax rules. The tax effects on their decisions can be more reliably identified and assessed.[24] The following briefly surveys empirical findings concerning the economic effects of international business taxation.

Location of Investments

Devereux and Griffith (1998) find empirical evidence that high tax rates reduce the probability that a country is chosen as an investment location by multinational companies. Overesch and Wamser (2009) provide empirical evidence that businesses more strongly react to taxes if investments are highly mobile. In accordance with profit-shifting considerations, subsidiaries of more internationalized companies are less tax responsive to host-country taxation. Huizinga and Voget (2009) empirically demonstrate that in case of cross-border mergers the new parent company is not located in countries with a high risk of international double taxation. Hebous, Ruf and Weichenrieder (2010) distinguish between greenfield investments and mergers and acquisitions (M&A). They find evidence that location choices of greenfield investment projects display higher tax sensitivity than M&A transactions. The tax response of M&A investments is significantly smaller. This finding points at a (partial) capitalization of taxes in the acquisition price when the investment project takes the form of an acquisition.

---

[24] Hines (1997).

Financing Decisions

Several empirical studies have analyzed the impact of taxes on the financing structure of multinational groups. Using data of U.S. multinational companies, Desai, Foley and Hines (2004) observe that internal debt reacts highly sensitive to taxation. Affiliates located in high-tax countries display higher internal debt than affiliates in low-tax countries. Huizinga, Laeven, and Nicodème (2008) find significant tax effects on capital structures of European multinational companies. Buettner, Overesch, Schreiber and Wamser (2009) analyze data of German multinationals and the tax response of internal debt and external debt. It turns out that internal debt responds more pronounced to taxes than external debt. The results are quantitatively in accordance with the results of Desai, Foley and Hines, suggesting that the U.S. credit system and the German exemption system have a similar impact on the capital structure of multinational companies.

Profit Shifting

Regarding international profit shifting, all empirical studies are confronted with the difficulty of separating the profit shifting channel under consideration from other possible profit shifting channels. Clausing (2003) compares prices settled in the case of U.S. intra-firm trade with prices uncontrolled parties are charged with. She identifies significant tax effects on product-level price data in the case of intra-firm sales whereas no tax response is found if sales to unrelated parties are considered. These results are supported by Grubert (2003), who observes that the ratio of intra-group transactions to total sales of U.S. affiliates is influenced by taxation. Schreiber and Overesch (2010) use German firm level data and analyze the impact of R&D on profit shifting through transfer prices. They find evidence for an increasing tax sensitivity of internal transactions with increasing R&D intensity. Tax planning through transfer prices does not affect profit shifting through debt financing. This suggests that the normal return on capital is shifted by debt financing whereas the economic rent is shifted by transfer prices.

A small number of empirical studies analyze real investment effects in high-tax countries which are associated with profit shifting activities. Grubert (2003) finds that U.S. multinational companies whose profit-shifting opportunities are higher than average, choose locations with either extremely low or extremely high tax levels. The preference for high-tax countries supports the view that, due to profit-shifting opportunities, multinational companies can benefit from competitive advantages. Overesch and Schreiber (2010) analyze how responsive investment decisions of multinational subsidiaries are to host-country taxes. The results suggest that the negative effect of the local tax rate on real investments is completely eliminated for industries with comparatively high amounts of firm-specific transactions. If part of the local profit is shifted away, it is effectively taxed at the tax rate imposed on an affiliated company. Thus, the tax level of affiliated companies also affects the investments. Overesch (2009) provides evidence that investment by foreign subsidiaries in the high-tax country Germany is negatively affected by tax rates of their parent companies.

Reading List Chapter 3

Büttner, Thies; Overesch, Michael; Schreiber, Ulrich; Wamser, Georg: Taxation and Capital Structure Choice - Evidence from a Panel of German Multinationals, in: Economics Letters 105(3), 2009, pp. 309-311.

Büttner, Thies; Overesch, Michael; Schreiber, Ulrich; Wamser, Georg: The Impact of Thin- Capitalization Rules on the Capital Structure of Multinational Firms, in: Journal of Public Economics, published online 13.07.12.

Clausing, Kimberly A.: The impact of transfer pricing on intra-firm trade, in: J.R. Hines (ed.), International taxation and multinational activity, Chicago, 2001, pp. 173-194.

Clausing, Kimberly A.: Tax-Motivated Transfer Pricing and US Intra-firm Trade Prices, Journal of Public Economics 2003, pp. 2207-2223.

Clausing, Kimberly A.: International tax avoidance and U.S. international trade, in: National Tax Journal 2006, pp. 269-287.

Desai, Mihir A.; Foley, Fritz; Hines, James R.: A Multinational Perspective on Capital Structure Choice and Internal Capital Markets, in: The Journal of Finance 2004, pp. 2451-2487.

Devereux, Michael P.; Griffith, Rachel: Taxes and the location of production: Evidence from a panel of US multinationals, in: Journal of Public Economics 1998, pp. 335-367.

Devereux Michael P.; Sørensen Peter B.: The corporate income tax: international trends and options for fundamental reform. Economic papers, Brussels, 2006.

Dixon, John; Finney, Malcolm (eds.): International Corporate Tax Planning, London, 2002.

Elschner, Christina; Spengel, Christoph: R&D Tax Incentives: Empirical Evidence, International Comparison and Reform Options for Germany, in: Zeitschrift für Betriebswirtschaft 2010 , Special Issue 2, pp. 1-22.

European Commission: European Tax Survey, Working Paper 3/2004, Office for Official Publications of the European Communities, Luxembourg, 2004.

Ernst & Young: Precision under Pressure - Global Transfer Pricing Survey 2007-2008, 2007.

Ernst & Young: 2009 Global Transfer Pricing Survey - Tax Authority Insights, Perspectives, Interpretations and Regulatory Changes, 2009.

Ewert, Ralf; Wagenhofer, Alfred: Interne Unternehmensrechung, 7th Edition, Heidelberg, 2008.

Finnerty, Chris; Merks, Paulus; Petriccione, Mario; Russo, Raffaele: Fundamentals of International Tax Planning, Amsterdam, 2007.

Grubert, Harry: Intangible Income, Intercompany Transactions, Income Shifting, and the Choice of Location, in: National Tax Journal 2003, pp. 221-242.

Hebous, Shafik; Ruf, Martin; Weichenrieder, Alfons: The Effects of Taxation on the Location Decisions of Multinational Firms: M&A vs. Greenfield Investments; CESifo Working Paper. 3076, 2010.

Hines, James: Lessons from the Behavioral Responses to International Taxation, in: National Tax Journal 1997, pp. 305 – 322.

Hirshleifer, Jack: On the Economics of Transfer Pricing, in: The Journal of Business 1956, pp. 172-184.

Huinzinga, Harry; Laeven, Luc; Nicodéme, Gaetan: Capital Structure and International Debt Shifting in Europe, in: Journal of Financial Economics 2008, pp. 80-118.

Huizinga, Harry; Voget, Johannes: International taxation and the direction and volume of cross-border M&As, in: Journal of Finance 2009, pp. 1217-1249.

Jog, Vijay; Tang, Jianmin: Tax Reforms, Debt Shifting and Tax Revenue: Multinational Corporations in Canada, in: International Tax and Public Finance 2001, pp. 5-25.

Miller, Angharad; Oats, Lynne: Principles of International Taxation, West Sussex, 2009.

Nocke, Volker; Yeaple, Stephen: An assignment theory of foreign direct investment, in: Review of Economic Studies 2008, pp. 529-557.

OECD: Transfer Pricing Guidelines for Multinational Enterprises and Tax Administrations 2010, Paris, 2010.

Overesch, Michael: The Effects of Multinationals´ Profit Shifting Activities on Real Investments, in: National Tax Journal 2009, pp. 5-23.

Overesch, Michael; Schreiber, Ulrich: Asset Specifity, International Profit Shifting, and Investment Decisions, in: Zeitschrift für Betriebswirtschaft 2010, Special Issue 2, pp. 23-47.

Overesch, Michael; Wamser, Georg: Who cares about Corporate Taxation? Asymmetric Tax Effects on Outbound FDI, in: World Economy 2009, pp. 1657-1684.

Raff, Horst; Ryan, Michael; Stähler, Frank: The choice of market entry mode: Greenfield investment, M&A and joint venture, in: International Review of Economics and Finance 2009, pp. 3-10.

Ruf, Martin: Why is the Response of Multinationals Capital Structure Choice to Tax Incentives That Low? Some Possible Explanations; in: Finanzarchiv 2011, pp. 123-144.

Schmalenbach, Eugen: Pretiale Wirtschaftslenkung, Volume 1, Die optimale Geltungszahl Bremen et al., 1947.

Scholes, Myron S.; Wolfson, Mark A.; Erickson, Merle; Maydew, Edward L.; Shevlin; Terry: Taxes and Business Strategy, 4th Edition; Upper Saddle River, New Jersey, 2009.

Schreiber, Ulrich; Führich, Gregor: European group taxation - the role of exit taxes, in: European Journal of Law and Economics 2009, S. 257-274.

Shackelford, Douglas A., Shevlin, Terry: Empirical tax research in accounting, in: Journal of Accounting and Economics 2001, pp. 321–387.

Zodrow, George R.: On the "Traditional" and "New" Views of Dividend Taxation, in: National Tax Journal 1991, pp. 497-509.

4. International Taxation and European Law

4.1. Fundamental Freedoms and Income Taxation

The Treaty on the Functioning of the European Union (TFEU) defines the internal market as an area without internal frontiers in which the free movements of goods, persons, services and capital is ensured (Art. 26 (2) TFEU).[25] For a true internal market, tax harmonization seems to be unavoidable. This is especially true for income taxes because international double taxation and international tax arbitrage both distort trade and investment patterns. Yet, European law only gives a mandate for the harmonization of indirect taxes, especially the value added tax (Art. 113 TFEU). As regards income taxes, Art. 115 TFEU provides the European Council with a mandate to issue directives concerning the approximation of laws affecting the functioning of the internal market. The council shall act unanimously (Art. 115 TFEU). Given the requirement of unanimity, income taxation is essentially still a matter for the individual Member States.

Fundamental Freedoms

Despite the EU Member States' far reaching tax autonomy, their tax law has to conform to European law. EU Member States design their tax law within the confines set by European primary law. Primary European law is supranational and ranks above national law. The relevant provisions are the fundamental economic freedoms: free movement of goods (Art. 28-32 TFEU), free movement of persons (Art. 45-48 TFEU), freedom of establishment (Art. 49-55 TFEU), freedom to provide services (Art. 56-62 TFEU), and free movement of capital and payments (Art. 63-66 TFEU). In the field of business taxation, the freedom of establishment and the free movement of capital are the most important. The case law of the European Court of Justice (ECJ), the court which interprets European law, has a growing influence on taxation in the European Union.

The fundamental freedoms are individual legal rights. Persons resident in the EU can invoke these legal rights (protected persons). Protected persons comprise EU citizens (Art. 49 TFEU) and legal persons (Art. 54 TFEU) resident in the EU. Legal persons protected by Art. 54 TFEU include, among others, incorporated business. However, the fundamental freedoms are only applicable on cross-border contexts (spatial scope).

---

25 Based on the agreement on the European Economic Area (EEA), the TFEU is also applicable to Iceland, Liechtenstein and Norway.

Preliminary Ruling Procedure

European law is exclusively interpreted by the ECJ to ensure a consistent application of EU law. The ECJ does not interpret national law. Interpretation of national law is a matter for the national courts. In the field of income tax, most legal action is started on a preliminary ruling proceeding. Under the set procedure, a national court can refer a case to the ECJ if it holds the view that the ruling of the ECJ on a point of community law is necessary for passing judging. The highest national court must refer a contentious point of European law to the ECJ as no further appeal is possible before national courts (Art. 267 TFEU). The right to refer a case at hand to the ECJ is restricted to the national courts of the Member States. The taxpayers (or government authorities) do not have the right to appeal directly to the ECJ.

If a tax rule is found not to conform to EU law, it can no longer be applied to EU citizens or EU companies. The rulings of the ECJ are binding precedents for all national courts and tax authorities involved in the actual case. Furthermore, a judgment by the ECJ is also binding on other Member States and their courts and tax authorities.

According to established case law, the ECJ assesses cases referred in a four step scheme. Firstly, it establishes whether one of the fundamental freedoms is relevant to the issue at hand, and if so, which one. Secondly, it establishes whether the relevant freedom is restricted or not. Thirdly, if the freedom is found to be restricted, the court must form a view on possible justifications. Fourthly, if a justification is accepted, it has to be in proportion to the purpose served.

4.2. Freedom of Establishment

4.2.1. Scope

The freedom of establishment includes the free choice of residence or seat and the free choice of setting up agencies, branches and subsidiaries in a foreign EU Member State. The freedom of establishment ensures the free choice of (self-employed) business activities within the territory of the EU. According to the ECJ, the freedom of establishment is relevant if there is a substantial or controlling interest in a company. In principle, a majority shareholding of 50% and more will be sufficient.[26] However, the definition offered by the tax rule at issue must also be taken into account. If, for example, a tax rule applies only to shareholdings exceeding 25%, the freedom of establishment is generally applicable because the tax rule under consideration is targeted at a controlling interest and not at portfolio investments (Lasertec, C-492/04).

The ECJ has also held that in the case of a controlling interest only the freedom of establishment applies whereas the free movement of capital and payments

[26] A shareholding of one third does not necessarily imply control of the company (Baars, C-251/98, lit. 20). A shareholding of 49% within a consortium is sufficient (ICI, C-264/98, lit. 5, 22).

is not to be considered. This is important because the freedom of establishment only applies to EU cases while the free movement of capital is applicable to investments (portfolio investments) in non-EU states as well. Member States' tax rules dealing with circumstances where a controlling interest is relevant have to respect for the freedom of establishment. As far as non-EU countries are involved, these rules need not, however, pass the test of fundamental freedoms as the freedom of capital and payments is not invoked.

4.2.2. Prohibited Restriction

In principle, it is forbidden to restrict the freedom of establishment. There is a ban on discrimination (Art. 56 TFEU), which covers cases where a foreign person invests in a Member State through a permanent establishment or a subsidiary (inbound cases). Overt discrimination because of citizenship or seat is forbidden. Covert discrimination by reference to factors other than citizenship or seat, but which leads to the same result as overt discrimination is forbidden as well.

Non-Restriction Approach

The ECJ has extended the discrimination ban to a general non-restriction approach developed from the Dassonville case (Dassonville, 8/74, lit. 5) and the Cassis de Dijon case (Cassis de Dijon, 120/78, lit. 8). The so-called Dassonville formula states that the principle of free trade prohibits all measures capable of hindering, directly or indirectly, actually or potentially, intra-community trade. According to the so-called Cassis de Dijon formula, there is no valid reason why goods, lawfully produced in one Member State, should not be introduced into any other Member State. Under the non-restriction approach, it is not allowed to impede a fundamental freedom by restricting it or making it less attractive. The restriction ban applies not only to inbound cases but to all cases where a resident person invests in another Member State either through a permanent establishment or a subsidiary (outbound cases). The same is true if a legal person transfers its seat to another Member State.

Transaction Based Comparison

Given this definition of non-restriction, each tax specifically targeted at a cross-border transaction could be seen as an unlawful restriction. Such a broad understanding of restriction would in effect imply full harmonization of European tax rules and regulations. As yet, the ECJ does not go so far. The non-restriction approach, regarding both inbound and outbound transactions, implies a comparison between similar transactions. The cross-border transaction is compared to a purely domestic transaction in terms of its tax treatment. If a tax treatment is less favorable, the taxpayer suffers from an objective disadvantage with respect to a cross-border transaction.

However, it cannot be inferred from European law that the tax effects of both domestic and foreign business activities should be neutral. Economic concepts of tax neutrality, such as financing neutrality or organizational form neutrality do not govern the court's judgments. More specifically, neither capital export neutrality nor capital import neutrality are legally relevant concepts. The ECJ requires comparability of cross-border transactions with domestic transactions in the light of a specific tax rule. For example, under the ECJ's approach, in general, a permanent establishment and a subsidiary are not comparable due to their different legal status and the different extent of tax liability. Therefore, the tax rules applicable to both legal forms may differ. On the other hand, the taxation of dividends received from a domestic corporation is comparable to the taxation of dividends received from a foreign corporation. Hence, the respective tax rules for both types of dividend have to be the same.

4.2.3. Justifications

A restriction may be justified. The treaty itself (Art. 52 TFEU) allows restrictions on the freedom of establishment if they are justified by reasons of either public policy, security or public health. However, the justifications explicitly mentioned in the treaty are usually not applicable in the area of income taxes. The ECJ has developed further justifications limiting the general ban on restricting freedoms. According to the rule of reason principle,[27] the ECJ demands for a justification of a national tax rule that the respective tax rule applies in a non-discriminatory manner, that the rule is justified by reasons of public interest, and that the rule is proportionate.

Rejected Justifications

The ECJ has considered several justifications brought forward by governments. The court has made clear which justifications can be accepted and which ones cannot be accepted. The following briefly describes the most important rejections of justifications for restrictions.

(i) Lacking harmonization of national tax law: national tax law must conform to European law. Otherwise, the missing tax harmonization would render the fundamental freedoms worthless. (ii) Reduction of tax revenue: fiscal reasons never justify a restriction. Otherwise, every restriction of a cross-border activity could be justified by a loss in tax revenue. (iii) Compensation of advantages: an unfavorable tax treatment of a taxpayer does not compensate for other advantages of the same taxpayer stemming from unrelated tax rules. The court has specified under which (specific) circumstances compensation is allowed. (iv) Tax administration: administrative problems in the taxation of cross-border activities do not justify a

[27] The rule of reason is an approach to interpret legal rules with conflicting goals, e.g. rules which promote free trade are evaluated against rules which restrict free trade in order to decide whether or not a trade practice should be prohibited.

restriction. The court points to the European Mutual Assistance Directive.[28] On the other hand, a Member State may impose an administrative burden on the taxpayer, e. g. for the purpose of rebutting an anti-abuse assumption. (v) Double taxation treaties: EU law is of higher rank than bilateral tax treaties. Therefore, the rules of a double taxation treaty cannot justify a restriction.

Accepted Justifications

The ECJ has accepted only a few justifications for restrictions. (i) Anti-avoidance rules: ensuring effective tax supervision is an accepted reason in the public interest. The fight against tax avoidance is, in principle, legitimate. (ii) Coherence: in general, coherence describes a situation where a number of different tax rules are systematically related to each other. The respective tax rules have to be in a systematic context in respect of the same taxpayer and the same tax. (iii) The allocation of power to impose taxes: Member States have to account for both profits and losses when exercising their taxing rights. Otherwise, a balanced allocation of the power to impose taxes between Member States would be jeopardized. Therefore taxpayers must not be free to choose where they are taxed.

4.2.4. Proportionality

An accepted justification has to be proportionate. This means that the following three criteria have to be met. (i) Appropriateness: a tax rule is appropriate if it ensures the attainment of the objective pursued. An anti-abuse rule, for example, is appropriate if it prevents abuse of the law. An anti-abuse rule is inappropriate if abuse still can occur despite the rule. (ii) Necessity: the tax rule may not go beyond what is necessary to attain the objective. There should be no less restrictive measure available. An anti-abuse rule is not necessary if it applies general criteria, e.g. if abuse is assumed without giving taxpayers the possibility to rebut the assumption. An anti-abuse rule which provides taxpayers with the opportunity to present sound business reasons for the transaction is less restrictive and still serves the objective of the anti-abuse rule. This criterion is regularly the decisive one for evaluating an accepted justification. (iii) Adequateness: a tax rule is adequate if the advantages from restricting a fundamental freedom exceed the disadvantages of the restricting tax rule. The last criterion is usually disregarded by the ECJ.

[28] Council Directive 2008/55/EC of 26 May 2008 on mutual assistance for the recovery of claims relating to certain levies, duties, taxes and other measures (OJ 2008 L 150, p. 28).

4.3. EU Law and International Tax Planning

4.3.1. Cross-Border Loss Compensation

4.3.1.1. Foreign Subsidiaries

If a foreign subsidiary incurs losses, international tax planning must cope with the fact that the losses are trapped there. On the other hand, some countries provide for group taxation rules offering a multinational group the opportunity to pool profits and losses at the country level. If foreign losses and foreign profits can be pooled, an immediate loss offset is achievable. However, as most group taxation schemes are restricted in terms of territoriality, loss compensation definitely has its limits. From the perspective of European law, the question arises if territorial restrictions on loss offset conform to the freedom of establishment.

Case Marks & Spencer

The ECJ had to decide this question in the case of a British based group (Marks & Spencer, C-446/03). Marks & Spencer (M&S) had established trading subsidiaries in Belgium, France and Germany. For several years, losses were incurred in all of these subsidiaries. The French subsidiary was sold. Trading operations of Belgian and German subsidiaries were terminated. In the residence countries of the subsidiaries, the losses could not be relieved for the lack of income. In the year in dispute, the British profits of M&S were high enough to completely absorb the foreign losses. M&S claimed surrender of the foreign losses to the domestic parent under the UK group relief rules. The British tax authority refused the claim as only domestic subsidiaries were eligible for group relief. M&S appealed against this decision to the courts, and the High Court referred the case to the ECJ.

The ECJ drew a comparison between a foreign and a domestic subsidiary. The court acknowledged a restriction of the freedom of establishment. Whereas the British group relief allows an immediate loss offset between domestic parent and domestic subsidiary, the parent cannot offset the loss of a foreign subsidiary. The foreign subsidiary can only carry forward its losses and, thus, suffers from cash flow and interest disadvantages. It becomes less attractive for a domestic parent to carry on business through foreign, rather than domestic, subsidiaries. An outbound discrimination is present against the foreign subsidiary because of the (foreign) seat of the company.

A restriction established by the exclusion of foreign losses must be justified. The ECJ accepted the exclusion of foreign losses if justified by a combination of the following three factors: (i) the balanced allocation of power to impose taxes, (ii) the prevention of a double dip, and (iii) the fight against tax avoidance. International groups must not be allowed an option as to where to be taxed on profits and where to claim losses. The exclusion of foreign losses prevents a double dip and is a reasonable measure to combat tax evasion.

However, losses may not be claimed by the foreign subsidiary if the loss carry forward is forfeited due to a change in ownership, liquidation or similar events.

When losses are ultimately forfeited in the residence state of a foreign subsidiary, the multinational group suffers from double taxation. Under such circumstances it is unacceptable for a Member State to prohibit the transfer of losses without exception. According to the ECJ, if the foreign loss cannot be claimed in the foreign state of residence any longer, relief must be available in the residence state of the parent. Unfortunately, the court did not provide a precise definition of an ultimately forfeit loss.

Consequences for Tax Planning

Although at first glance, international tax planning with respect to foreign losses seems to be limited, there is room for maneuver. Multinationals have an incentive to claim foreign losses in a high-tax jurisdiction, while being taxed on foreign profits in a low-tax jurisdiction. Usually specific measures will be necessary to shift the loss to a high-taxed parent. Various tax planning strategies may be feasible. Restructuring the foreign subsidiary may hinder the utilization of a loss carry-forward. If a subsidiary is liquidated, the loss carry-forward ceases with the legal person itself. The subsidiary may be merged into a partnership or another corporation and, as a result, forfeit its loss carry-forward. Finally, the ownership of the subsidiary could be changed by selling or transferring the shareholding to another group member. A change in ownership may eliminate the loss carry-forward of the subsidiary.[29]

Of course, legal restrictions on tax planning have to be taken into account. Member States could implement anti-abuse legislation focusing on transactions which are solely motivated by tax reasons. According to ECJ case law, however, anti-abuse legislation must not be too general in scope. Loss deduction in the parent's state of residence cannot be prevented if there are sound business reasons for the liquidation or restructuring of the subsidiary. This can be assumed in the case of subsidiaries suffering permanent losses.

4.3.1.2. Foreign Permanent Establishments

In the case of a foreign permanent establishment, the loss is trapped in the permanent establishment if the investor´s country of residence applies the exemption method to avoid international double taxation. Countries applying the exemption method neither tax foreign profits nor do they allow the deduction of foreign losses. Under these rules, it is impossible for the investor to pool domestic profits and foreign losses to achieve an immediate loss offset. However, the foreign loss may be carried forward in the foreign country, despite both cash flow and interest disadvantages.

---

29 See Sec. 8c Corporation Tax Act (KStG) in the German case.

Case Lidl Belgium

The ECJ had to deal with a foreign permanent establishment's losses (Lidl Belgium, C-414/06). Lidl Belgium claimed the deduction of losses originating in a Luxembourg permanent establishment from the German tax base. This was not accepted by the German fiscal authorities because business profits derived from a permanent establishment were exempted under the double taxation treaty. The German Supreme Tax Court referred the case to the ECJ.

As in the Marks & Spencer case, the freedom of establishment applied. There was outbound discrimination because the foreign losses could not be claimed in the state of residence, whereas domestic losses could be deducted without any restriction. Yet, outbound discrimination was justified by the allocation of power to impose taxes and the prevention of a double dip. Based on the Marks & Spencer judgment, the ECJ decided that only if the foreign loss is final, can it be claimed in the residence state of the investor. The loss cannot be claimed if a loss carry-forward is still available in the state where the permanent establishment is located.

Consequences for Tax Planning

The tax planning consequences are basically the same as in the case of foreign subsidiaries. For both foreign subsidiaries and foreign permanent establishments, it is possible to account for losses in the investor's residence state if foreign loss relief is forfeited. Again, tax planning focuses on the conditions which determine the forfeit of the foreign loss. Tax planning may be facilitated if Member States tighten their loss compensation rules. Member States with low income tax rates tend to have strict loss compensation rules (in particular restrictions in time are observable), while Member States with comparably high income tax rates apply more generous loss compensation rules. Given this setting, losses from low tax jurisdictions may be claimed in high tax jurisdictions without facing the allegation of tax avoidance.

On the other hand, the German Supreme Tax Court has held that cases where loss relief is curtailed due to restrictions in foreign tax law are not covered by the ECJ's ruling. The German court ruled that losses of a foreign permanent establishment which could no longer be deducted due to a restriction on the loss carry-forward cannot be regarded as finally forfeited (BFH, I R 100/09). As opposed to legal restrictions, which are disregarded by the court, factual reasons are accepted. A factual reason for the forfeit of a foreign loss could be the reorganization of the permanent establishment (e.g. merger or liquidation). If the factual reasons are given, the investor's state of residence has to give relief for the final foreign loss.

4.3.2. Dividend Taxation

Individual shareholders of a foreign corporation face both the foreign corporation tax and the domestic individual income tax on dividends. If the foreign corporation is held through a domestic corporation, the domestic corporation, as a rule, receives the foreign dividends tax-free. Individual income tax is due upon redistribution of the dividends to the domestic corporation's individual shareholders. From a European law perspective, it has to be established whether the taxation of foreign dividends conforms to the fundamental freedoms.

Case Manninen

The case before the ECJ concerned the taxation of foreign dividends within an imputation system (Manninen, C-319/02). Mr. Manninen, subject to unlimited tax liability in Finland, received dividends from a Swedish corporation. In Finland, corporate profits and capital income, including dividends, were taxed at 29% at the time of the proceedings, against an income tax credit of 29/71. Effectively, dividends were exempt from the individual income tax.[30] However, the tax credit was restricted to domestic dividends. The Swedish dividends were taxed at a rate of 29% and only the Swedish withholding tax of 15% was credited. Mr. Manninen appealed to the Finnish High Administrative Court which referred the case to the ECJ.

The specific Finnish tax rule granted the imputation tax credit to all shareholders of domestic corporations. Hence the free movement of capital was applicable. The ECJ made a comparison between a shareholding in a domestic company and a shareholding in a foreign company. The Finnish tax imputation system disadvantaged the recipient of foreign dividends over his domestic counterpart. Therefore, there was an outbound discrimination. Finnish individuals faced a tax obstacle when they acquired foreign shares. Investments in foreign companies were less attractive than investments in domestic companies. It was also more difficult for Swedish companies to raise capital in Finland due to the additional tax burden compared to domestic shareholdings.

The suggested justification lay in the coherence of the Finnish tax system. The tax imputation system is characterized by an advantage (tax credit for the natural person) and a disadvantage (profits of the corporation are taxed), which seems to be coherent. However, the objective of the credit system is the removal of economic double taxation, which is obviously not achieved, unless the tax credit is granted irrespective of the tax residence of the company distributing the profits. Thus, the ECJ did not accept coherence as a justification for the infringement of free capital movement.

Finland reacted to the judgment and replaced its imputation system by a shareholder relief system.[31] The former German corporation imputation tax system was similarly challenged by the ECJ (Meilicke, C-292/04). However, before judgment was given, Germany replaced its imputation tax system with a shareholder relief system. Other Member States, in particular France, Italy and the United Kingdom, have also replaced their imputation tax systems with shareholder relief systems.

---

30 Because interest income was taxed at 29%, the Finnish corporate tax system was neutral with respect to new equity financing and debt financing.

31 As dividends are taxed twice, whereas interest income is only taxed once, the shareholder relief system is not neutral with respect to financing decisions.

Consequences for Tax Planning

From a corporate tax planning perspective, the ECJ's rulings concerning dividend taxation may not be considered very important. Publicly held corporations usually do not have information about the tax status of their shareholders and, thus, do not take individual income taxes into account. Many shareholders face a shareholder relief system which taxes dividends irrespective of their origin. Under these conditions, the management of publicly held corporations may reasonably neglect the individual income tax consequences of investment decisions. A corporation choosing, for example, to invest in a foreign low-tax jurisdiction increases its net profits and, at the same time, acts in the interest of all shareholders subjected to a shareholder relief system because a shareholder relief system creates no "home-bias". A higher after-tax profit of the corporation results in a higher after-tax dividend, irrespective of the profit's origin.

4.3.3. Debt Financing

4.3.3.1. Internal Debt Financing

Although interest payments have to conform to the dealing at arm's length standard, profits can be shifted to affiliates located in low-tax jurisdictions by increasing internal loans granted to high-taxed affiliates. However, multinationals face restrictions on the deductibility of interest payments related to internal loans. Thin capitalization (TC) rules limit the amount of tax effective internal loans. Tight TC rules are a major obstacle to international profit shifting through internal debt. TC rules, however, may infringe on European law, in particular on the freedom of establishment.

Case Lankhorst-Hohorst

The ECJ case on TC rules was the German case of Lankhorst-Hohorst GmbH, C-324/00. Lankhorst-Hohorst GmbH, resident in Germany, suffered from an accumulated deficit exceeding equity capital. Its sole shareholder, the Dutch Lankhorst-Hohorst BV, was wholly owned by the Dutch Lankhorst Taselaar BV. The latter granted a loan to the German GmbH. This was intended as a substitute for equity capital and accompanied by a comfort letter. The German tax authorities reclassified the interest payments of the German corporation as a hidden profit distribution according to the then valid German TC rules. Lankhorst-Hohorst GmbH appealed to the tax court of first instance, which referred the case to the ECJ.

The ECJ made a comparison between a German parent with a German subsidiary and a foreign parent with a German subsidiary. Even though German TC rules did not openly entail discrimination on the basis of nationality, the fact remained that a foreign shareholder was always subjected to German TC rules whereas German shareholders were subjected to these rules only in exceptional circumstances. Effectively there was a systematic difference in treatment between resident companies with domestic and foreign shareholders. This was a case of covert inbound discrimination. The German TC rules therefore violated the freedom of establishment.

The justification of fighting tax evasion was not accepted by the ECJ. As opposed to an anti-abuse rule, the legislation at issue did not have the specific purpose of preventing wholly artificial arrangements designed to circumvent German tax legislation. It applied generally to any situation in which the parent company had its seat outside Germany. Furthermore, there was no abuse through an artificial contractual arrangement in the actual case, because the loan had been granted to financially support the German corporation.

Consequences for Tax Planning

The court's ruling greatly facilitated international tax planning through internal debt financing. TC rules targeted at cross-border internal loans now conflict European law. Germany and other Member States with comparable rules have reacted accordingly, though not in a uniform manner. Various possibilities were open to Member States, including abolition of TC rules, the modification of those rules towards a purely anti-abusive measure, or extension of the rules to include domestic shareholders. The first solution clearly would have endangered tax revenue. The second solution probably would have had the same effect, given the narrow scope of purely anti-abuse rules. The German legislative, at that time, chose to extend the TC rules to domestic shareholders.

TC rules that conform with European law can effectively curb abuses from cross-border internal debt financing. However, their effect can be much wider than originally intended, as in the German case, where domestic financing decisions are also restricted. The German attempt to relieve some of the worse results of the extension to domestic debt by relaxing the TC rules for domestic group companies,[32] raises other doubts on conformity with European law.

4.3.3.2. External Debt Financing

Multinationals may not only make use of internal debt financing to reduce the tax burden of the group. External debt financing can generate a tax shield in a high tax jurisdiction as well. In particular, a corporate parent located in a high-tax country can take up a loan and use the proceeds to re-finance the acquisition of a corporation located in a low-tax country. In effect, the interest payments may trigger domestic corporate tax savings which exceed the corporation tax payments on the foreign profits. It does not come as a surprise that Member States are inclined to restrict international tax rate arbitrage of this kind. However, such restrictions are challenged by European law.

---

[32] See Sec. 4h Income Tax Act (EStG) and Sec. 15 no. 3 Corporation Act (KStG).

Case Bosal

The ECJ dealt with restrictions on interest deductibility (Bosal, C-168/01). Bosal Holding BV was a corporation resident in the Netherlands. The corporation received dividends from subsidiaries located in various EU Member States. The dividends were tax-free in the Netherlands. Bosal incurred management and finance costs for the foreign holdings, which were, in principle, deductible expenses. However, there was a restriction on the tax deductibility of expenses related to tax-exempted foreign earnings. Bosal appealed to the Hoge Raad which referred the case to the ECJ.

The ECJ compared a domestic parent with a foreign subsidiary to a domestic parent with a domestic subsidiary. Deduction of management and finance costs relating to domestic income was allowed, whereas deduction was disallowed for the same costs relating to foreign income. The foreign subsidiary itself could not deduct the costs either because the parent had incurred the expenses. Therefore, deductibility of the respective costs within the group was not possible. The court ruled that an outbound discrimination was present against the parent with a foreign subsidiary. It became less attractive for the parent to carry on business through foreign subsidiaries then through domestic subsidiaries. The tax rules at issue violated the freedom of establishment.

From the perspective of the Netherlands' income tax, non-deductibility of expenses which are related to tax-free income is a necessary element of the income tax law and, thus, the Netherlands maintained that the tax rules in question were coherent. The court, though, did not accept the argument because two taxpayers were involved. Moreover, there was no direct advantage to compensate the disadvantage of disallowing the deduction of costs. On the contrary, the refusal to deduct costs resulted in double taxation.

Consequences for Tax Planning

The ECJ's ruling does not only prevent the risk of double taxation, it greatly facilitates international tax arbitrage. In particular, debt financed acquisitions of foreign corporations can be tax-efficient structured by allocating the loan to a high-taxed group company which acquires the shares of the corporation. The interposition of a holding company which takes up the loan can serve the same purpose.

In Germany, the legislative reacted to international debt tax planning opportunities by amending the Income Tax Act and introducing a comprehensive interest stripping rule covering both internal and external debt financing.[33] The German TC rules accept a debt-equity ratio which is equal to or less as the group's overall debt-equity ratio. If the group's leverage falls short of the leverage of the German group company, debt capital has to be relocated from Germany to group companies resident in other countries and be replaced by the same amount of equity

[33] See Sec. 4h Income Tax Act (EStG), enacted in 2008. Exception clauses are targeted at small and medium sized businesses as well as to businesses operating on a stand-alone basis.

capital. Multinational groups' tax planning must ensure that debt which is transferred to non-German group members does not face restrictions and generates sufficient tax savings in its new environment.

With respect to cross-border debt financing, the German interest stripping rule seems to be effective. It covers all types of debt, it prevents a switch from internal loans to external loans, thereby restricting multinational groups' ability to implement debt in Germany.

4.3.4. Income Tax Deferral

Multinationals can take advantage of low statutory corporation tax rates by transferring financial assets to a low-taxed subsidiary. The subsidiary may engage in the group's cash pooling (finance company). A finance company may invest its funds at the capital market or it may grant loans to companies belonging to the group. In both cases, the finance company generates low-taxed profits if it is located in a country which provides either a low corporation tax rate or a special tax regime for finance companies. Finance companies can also be used to borrow capital from the capital market and to distribute the proceeds as internal debt to other group members. The finance company earns a profit margin if the interest income exceeds the interest paid to external lenders. The profit margin is low-taxed. Finance companies often face the restrictions of controlled foreign corporations (CFC) legislation. However, CFC legislation is under challenge at European law.

Case Cadbury Schweppes

The ECJ dealt with CFC legislation (Cadbury Schweppes, C-194/04). Cadbury Schweppes a parent company resident in the UK had shareholdings in the UK, other Member States and non-EU states, among them two Irish subsidiaries, which were subject to a tax rate of 10%. The Irish subsidiaries' business was to raise finance and to provide the funds to other group members. The low-taxed profits of the Irish subsidiaries were subject to British CFC legislation. Cadbury Schweppes appealed to the national court, which referred the case to the ECJ.

The ECJ compared a domestic parent with a foreign subsidiary to a domestic parent with a domestic subsidiary. Foreign and domestic subsidiaries are comparable as tax deferral is a result of the fact that the corporation is a legally distinct entity. CFC legislation, however, referred only to foreign subsidiaries. There was outbound discrimination against the domestic parent with a foreign subsidiary which violated the freedom of establishment. It became less attractive for a shareholder to carry on business through foreign subsidiaries than through domestic entities.

The ECJ accepted the fight against tax evasion as a justification for CFC legislation. However, the specific objective of CFC legislation must be to prevent the creation of wholly artificial arrangements which do not reflect economic reality. General criteria such as the tax residence of the corporation, the corporation tax rate and the classification of the earned income are not suitable criteria for the determination of abuse. CFC legislation as an anti-abuse measure is not proportionate if such general criteria apply. Taxpayers must have the possibility to rebut an abuse assumption by providing evidence that a genuine economic activity is being pursued through a properly equipped fixed establishment. If taxpayers can show this, their tax-saving motives become irrelevant.

Consequences for Tax Planning

ECJ case law greatly facilitates multinational groups' tax planning in this area. As finance companies usually are not wholly artificial arrangements but perform well defined economic functions, CFC legislation cannot obtain its objective to make it unattractive to establish such companies in a low-tax Member State. Various possibilities of reacting to ECJ case law are available to the Member States, including abolition of the CFC legislation altogether and its redesign as a specific anti-abuse provision. Germany has amended the CFC rules to disaplly them if taxpayers provide evidence that the foreign corporation engages in a genuine economic activity in a foreign Member State.[34]

Although an anti-abuse provision is less far reaching than the abolition of CFC legislation, it can have more or less the same effect on the multinational's tax planning opportunities and a Member State's tax revenue. Given the strict requirements set on anti-abuse rules, a specific rule may be inappropriate to effectively combat tax planning by means of finance companies. According to the ECJ, genuine economic activity implies a minimum of staff and equipment, sufficient to perform the functions involved. A highly mobile economic function, such as financing, does not need much staff and equipment. The transfer of the function is not very costly and the legal requirements concerning staff and equipment may be fulfilled anyway. Therefore, a multinational group will usually be able to present numerous evidence of a finance company's genuine economic activity.

4.3.5. Outbound Transfer of Assets

An important field of international tax planning is the cross-border restructuring of a group. Restructuring may take place in the form of a cross-border merger, a cross-border transfer of assets in exchange for shares or the cross-border transfer of a corporation´s seat. In all those cases, assets may be transferred from one Member State to another. As the tax accounting rules of all Member States are based on historical acquisition cost and the realization principle, hidden reserves (the difference between market value and tax book value of an asset) may be transferred to another jurisdiction. A Member State's tax claim to hidden reserves may be restricted or even completely lost by the transfer of the reserves. To prevent a loss in tax revenue, states have implemented exit taxation rules. Under such rules, transferred hidden reserves are taxed when they leave a jurisdiction. However, exit taxation rules potentially infringe European law.

---

[34] See Sec. 8 (2) Foreign Tax Act (AStG).

Case National Grid Indus BV

The ECJ has dealt with exit taxation regarding business assets (National Grid Indus BV, C-371/10). National Grid Indus, a limited liability company incorporated under Netherlands law, transferred its place of effective management to the United Kingdom and, as a result, according to the applicable double tax treaty was deemed to be resident in the United Kingdom. Only the United Kingdom was entitled to tax the profits and capital gains after the transfer of the tax residence. The Netherlands taxed the hidden reserves (unrealized gains) upon the transfer of the assets.

In accordance with Article 54 TFEU, companies are to be treated in the same way as natural persons who are nationals of Member States. A company incorporated under the law of a Member State which transfers its tax residence to another Member State, without losing its status of a company of the Member State of origin, may invoke the freedom of establishment (Article 49 TFEU).

The ECJ compared a cross-border transfer of seat to a national transfer of seat. In the latter case, the Netherlands did not tax the hidden reserves (capital gains) relating to the assets of a company until they were realized. The Court stated that the tax burden on unrealized profits on a cross-border transfer of seat had the potential to deter a company from transferring its place of management to another Member State. Such a company suffers from a disadvantage in terms of cash flow. The difference of treatment between cross-border transfer of seat and domestic transfer of seat constitutes a prohibited restriction of the freedom of establishment.

A restriction of the freedom of establishment can be justified by the preservation of the balanced allocation of powers of taxation between the Member States. The Member State of origin needs not abandon its right to tax hidden reserves which arose in its territory before the transfer and is, thus, entitled to tax the hidden reserves accumulated at the time of the exit. Otherwise a Member States right to comprehensively tax profits would be jeopardized. Profits earned after the transfer of seat are taxed exclusively in the new host Member State. These rules avoid double taxation of profits.

In order to assess the proportionality of immediate exit taxation, the Court made a distinction between the establishment of the amount of tax and its collection. A Member State may definitely determine the tax due on the hidden reserves that have arisen in its territory at the time of exit. The Member State of origin is not obliged to account for fluctuations in value that occur after the transfer of assets. The Member State of destination will in principle take account of the transferred assets' profits and losses. Yet, immediate exit taxation is disproportionate. Deferred exit taxation would not endanger the allocation of powers of taxation between the Member States, and it would be a less restrictive measure because deferred exit taxation avoids the cash flow disadvantages of immediate exit taxation. The Member State of origin may address the risk of non-recovery of the tax by the provision of a bank guarantee.

Under a regime of deferred exit taxation, transferred assets must be traced until realization. Organizing such tracing in case of a complex asset situation could involve high compliance and administrative costs. High compliance cost could be seen as a hindrance to the freedom of establishment that could be as harmful as immediate exit taxation. Against this background, the Court concluded that exit taxation rules offering a company the choice between immediate payment of the amount of tax with its cash flow disadvantage or deferred payment with its administrative disadvantage, would be less harmful. According to the ECJ, tracing of assets does not impose an excessive administrative burden on the Member States' tax administrations. In this context, the Court pointed to the Mutual Assistance Directive.[35]

Consequences for Tax Planning

A multinational group's tax planning follows from actions taken by Member States. Various choices are available to Member States, among them the abolition of exit taxation or the introduction of fair value tax accounting. Abolition of exit taxation is fiscally not feasible, given the tax planning opportunities and the high tax revenue losses to be expected. Fair value tax accounting solves the problem. Hidden reserves cannot accrue because all assets are currently valued at market value and unrealized profits are taxed. Yet, current values are hard to establish if market prices do not exist (which is usually the case for business assets) undermining the legal certainty of income taxation.

Given the ECJ ruling in the National Grid Indus case, Member States may establish a deferred taxation regime for the cross-border transfer of hidden reserves. However, it is difficult for the tax authorities to obtain information about the whereabouts of assets and the time of realization. Administrative problems particularly arise, if assets are transferred within the EU or if taxpayers move within the EU. Moreover, the lack of coordination and harmonization may lead to non-taxation of hidden reserves. Hidden reserves are not taxed if assets leave the tax base in the Member State of origin at book value and enter the tax base in the new Member State of residence at market value.

Simplified deferred exit taxation schemes could be considered by Member States in order to avoid the complexities of exit taxation based on actual realization. The tax burden would still be determined upon the exit of assets. While current assets could be immediately taxed, the exit tax of fixed assets could be assessed and deferred based on asset specific tax deferral rules. Tax deferral rules could be implemented in accordance with depreciation schedules to apportion hidden reserves and related tax payments to fiscal years following the year of exit. Interest and cash flow disadvantages could be avoided without creating excessive compliance and administrative costs. However, ECJ case law requires that all assumptions on which a tax deferral regime is based must be subject to rebuttal by the taxpayer.

Whatever exit taxation regime the Member States may establish, exit tax planning is greatly facilitated. Cash flow and interest disadvantages from the cross-border transfer of assets are to a large extent removed if exit taxes can be deferred.

---

[35] Council Directive 2008/55/EC of 26 May 2008 on mutual assistance for the recovery of claims relating to certain levies, duties, taxes and other measures (OJ 2008 L 150, p. 28).

Reading List Chapter 4

Brosens, Linda: Thin Capitalization Rules and EU Law, in: EC Tax Review 2004, pp. 188-213.

Cordewener; Axel; Pistone, Pasquale; Reimer, Ekkehart; Romano, Carlo: The Tax Treatment of Foreign Losses: Ritter, M&S, and the Way ahead, in: European Taxation, 2004; pp. 135-142; pp. 218-233.

Führich, Gregor: Exit Taxation and ECJ case law, in: European Taxation 2008, pp. 10-19.

Gammie, Malcolm: The Role of the European Court of Justice in the Development of Direct Taxation in the European Union, in: Bulletin for International Fiscal Documentation 2003, pp. 86-98.

Helminen, Marjaana: Is there a Future for CFC-Regimes in the EU?, in: International Tax review 2005, pp. 117-123.

Koch, Reinald; Spengel, Christoph; Oestreicher, Andreas: How to Reform Taxation of Corporate Groups in Europe, in: World Tax Journal 2011, pp. 5-38.

Lang, Michael, Aigner, Hans-Jörgen; Scheuerle, Ulrich; Stefaner, Markus: CFC Legislation – Domestic Provisions, Tax Treaties and EC Law, Vienna, 2004.

Lang, Michael; Pistone, Pasquale; Schuch, Josef; Staringer, Claus: Introduction to European Tax Law on Direct Taxation, 2nd Edition, Vienna, 2010.

Meussen, Gerard: The Principle of Equality in European Taxation, London, 1999.

Meussen, Gerard: Cross-Border Loss Compensation, and Permanent Establishments: Lidl Belgium and Deutsche Shell, in: European Taxation 2008, pp. 233-236.

Miller, Angharad; Oats, Lynne: Principles of International Taxation, West Sussex, 2009.

Peeters, Bruno: The Concept of Tax, EATLP Congress 2005, Naples, 2005.

Schreiber, Ulrich; Führich, Gregor: European group taxation – the role of exit taxes; in: European Journal of Law and Economics 2009, pp. 257-274.

Terra, Ben J.M.; Wattel, Peter J.; European Tax Law 5th Edition, Alphen aan den Rijn, 2008.

European Court of Justice:

Dassonville	8/74	ECR 1974	pp. 837 -866
Daily Mail	81/87	ECR 1988	pp. 5483-5514
Bachmann	C-204/90	ECR I-1992	pp. 249-286
Schumacker	C-279/93	ECR I-1995	pp. 225-268
Gebhard	C-55/94	ECR I-1995	pp. 4165-4201
Asscher	C-107/94	ECR I-1996	pp. 3089-3132
Leur-Blom	C-28/95	ECR I-1997	pp. 4161-4208
Futura	C-250/95	ECR I-1997	pp. 2471-2506
Saint-Gobain	C-307/97	ECR I-1999	pp. 6161-6206

Verkooijen	C-35/98	ECR I-2000	pp. 4071-4137
Metallgesellschaft	C-397/98	ECR I-2001	pp. 1727-1794
Metallgesellschaft	C-410/98	ECR I-2001	pp. 1727-1794
Amid	C-141/99	ECR I-2000	pp. 11619-11645
Lankhorst-Hohorst	C-324/00	ECR I-2002	pp. 11779-11817
Bosal	C-168/01	ECR I-2003	pp. 9409-9447
De Lasteyrie du Saillant	C-9/02	ECR I-2004	pp. 2409-2460
Manninen	C-319/02	ECR I-2004	pp. 7477-7515
Marks & Spencer	C-446/03	ECR I-2005	pp. 10837-10886
Cadburry Schweppes	C-194/04	ECR I-2006	pp. 7995-8054
Meilicke	C-292/04	ECR I-2007	pp. 1835-1890
Oy AA	C-231/05	ECR I-2007	pp. 6373-6414
Lidl Belgium	C-414/06	ECR I-2008	pp. 3601-3634
National Grid Indus BV	C-371/10		

German Federal Fiscal Court:

BFH	I R 100/09	BStB II 2010	p. 1065

5. Corporate Tax Harmonization in the European Union

5.1. Common Consolidated Corporate Tax Base

A European group faces many different tax systems. The group's profit is allocated to the Member States where the group has taxable activities on the basis of separate entity accounting and the arm's length principle. Profit determination according to the different tax codes of the Member States as well as profit allocation by transfer prices can entail double taxation caused by overlapping tax bases as well as high compliance and administrative costs. In the view of the European Community these are the major tax obstacles to the full realization of the internal market. Doing business in Europe should neither be distorted by taxes nor should it entail additional compliance and administrative costs.

Group Taxation

The European Commission proposes a European group taxation scheme, referred to as the common consolidated corporate tax base (CCCTB). Taxation would no longer depend on either separate entity accounting or on the arm's length principle, but would be based on common European tax accounting rules.[36] The CCCTB is an optional and additional tax code with common rules for all participating Member States. It aims at eliminating tax planning measures generated by separate entity accounting, in particular with respect to loss offset, debt financing and intra-group transactions.

The adoption of CCCTB would neither affect nor abolish any of the existing Member States' tax codes. If the parent company of a group opts for CCCTB, the group is bound for a minimum of five years. Corporations opting for CCCTB have to apply its rules for all their EU businesses (all-in or all-out option). The CCCTB regime is restricted to the European part of a group or to the Member States adopting CCCTB should it not be implemented in all Member States. With respect to group companies in non-EU countries, separate entity accounting and the established OECD-rules will continue to apply.

The consolidated profit of a European group is allocated to the group companies under CCCTB rules. Profit allocation is based on certain economic factors

[36] European Commission, Proposal for a Council Directive on a Common Consolidated Corporate Tax Base (CCCTB), Brussels COM (2011) 212/4.

(formula apportionment) and offers full consolidation of all intra-group transactions. Thus, the group's tax base does not include intra-group profits. CCCTB is not targeted at harmonization of the statutory tax rates. The Member States tax their share of the group profit at their own corporation tax rates.

Common Tax Base

Member States must agree upon a set of common rules determining the tax base of corporations under the CCCTB regime. The European Financial Reporting Standards (endorsed IFRS) provide a common legal terminology, which follows from the previous harmonization of accounting law. However, financial accounting rules are not appropriate to determine a tax base without modification. IFRS are designed to provide information to capital markets. Tax accounting rules, on the other hand, serve the purpose to determine an annual tax payment based on profit. If taxes were determined on the basis of financial accounts, the application of IFRS would become tax-driven to the detriment of the provision of useful information.

Fair value accounting, in particular, which is important for financial accounting, is unsuitable for tax purposes. Companies would pay taxes on unrealized profits. As opposed to fair value accounting, historical cost accounting and the realization principle ensure that companies have liquid funds available when they have to pay taxes. In any case, the necessary estimation of fair values based on cash flows and discount rates implies considerable legal uncertainty and increased risk of litigation. Therefore, it is not surprising that the tax accounting rules proposed by the European Commission build on historical cost accounting and the realization principle.

Apportionment of the Tax Base

Because the CCCTB is based on a formula apportionment, the consolidated profit of the group has to be attributed to the Member States where the group has taxable activities, i.e. where the group has established subsidiaries or permanent establishments and is thus subject to unlimited or limited tax liability. Corporations and permanent establishments, although different from a legal perspective, are treated equally under the CCCTB. A formula apportionment is usually based on allocation factors such as capital, labor and sales. Such a three factor formula reflects the factors of production as well as the marketing activities of a group. In the event of an overall loss, every Member State has to absorb its share of loss according to the same formula.

Tax Administration and Tax Compliance

A European group opting for CCCTB deals with one tax administration and is subject to a single set of tax rules. Compared to the current situation, this generally entails a reduction of tax compliance costs. On the other hand, because a new set of rules is added to those existing, tax compliance costs may even increase. This applies in particular to a multinational group facing the CCCTB regime within the EU as well as the separate entity accounting regime in other countries.

Because the assessment and allocation of the CCCTB group's tax base is the sole responsibility of the Member State where the group's parent is resident, a high degree of administrative cooperation between Member States is necessary. Information must be exchanged and close cooperation is needed if, for example, tax audits are to be performed. Even if Member States agree on far reaching cooperation, problems still remain. The fact that a single Member State is responsible for the tax base assessment of the group may create an incentive for this Member State's tax administration to be perceived as more lenient than other Member States' tax authorities in order to attract the headquarters of European groups.

5.2. Profit Allocation

5.2.1. Scope of the Group and Determination of Profits

Criteria to determine the scope of a group can be based on economic or legal considerations. The U.S. Unitary Taxation, which is comparable to CCCTB, uses tests which are predominantly based on economic criteria, such as centralized management, intra-group transactions and the allocation of business functions. The U.S. experience reveals that facts based on economic criteria, although they are adequate to determine economic units, are hard to observe and to assess for the taxing authorities. The legal uncertainty inherent in vague economic criteria triggers high compliance and administrative costs, provides the groups with tax planning incentives, and increases the risk of dispute. Legal criteria, such as the shareholding quota, may not be fully adequate to indicate the existence of an integrated group, but a shareholding quota is easily observable and applicable by taxing authorities.

Scope of the Group

In financial accounting, affiliates are included in consolidated statements if they are controlled by the parent. This is usually assumed when the shareholding exceeds 50%. The CCCTB participation threshold should, however, be higher in order to curb tax planning opportunities. A low participation threshold makes it easy for a group to include an affiliate such as when losses are expected. A high participation threshold takes into account that group taxation based on a formula allocation implies a high degree of economic integration of the group's companies. The membership of the group is thus more difficult to manipulate.

The European Commission´s proposal for a council directive (CCCTB-PCD) includes all subsidiaries if the parent owns (directly or indirectly) more than 50% of the voting rights and more than 75% of the capital. Shareholding criteria are irrelevant if the parent participates in more than 75% of the subsidiary´s profits (Art. 54 CCCTB-PCD).

Example (5.1): G Corporation, located in Germany, owns 60% of the voting rights and 80% of the capital of N Corporation, located in the Netherlands, and 30% of the shares in S corporation, located in Spain. G Corporation also owns 40% of the voting rights of F Corporation, located in France; G Corporation participates in 80% of F Corporations profit. G Corporation acquired all shareholdings in the same year. If G Corporation opts for the CCCTB, the subsidiary N is part of the CCCTB group because the respective share of voting rights and capital exceed the quota of 50% and 75%. F Corporation is also part of the CCCTB group because G Corporation has a claim to more than 75% of F Corporation´s profit. As a result, the group corporations G, N and F have to apply the common profit determination rules and the group's profit is allocated to Germany, the Netherlands and Italy via the agreed formula. S Corporation is not a CCCTB group company because the shareholding falls short of the participation threshold.

Tax Accounting Rules

The most important tax accounting rules incorporated in the European Commission´s proposed council directive are: Profits and losses are recognized only when realized and transactions are measured individually (Art. 9 CCCTB-PCD). The tax base is calculated as revenues less expenses (Art. 10 CCCTB-PCD) on an accrual basis (Art. 17 CCCTB-PCD). Revenues accrue when the right to receive the revenues arises, regardless of deferral of the actual payment (Art. 18 CCCTB-PCD). Deductible expenses are incurred if the obligation to make the payment has arisen and if the significant risks and rewards of ownership have been transferred to the taxpayers (Art. 19 CCCTB-PCD). If a probable future legal obligation is probable, any amount arising from that obligation is deductible (provision), provided that the eventual settlement of the amount is expected to result in a deductible expense (Art. 25 CCCTB-PCD).

The difference in the value of stocks and work-in-progress at the beginning and end of the year and is tax-deductible (Art. 21 CCCTB-PCD). The costs of stock and work-in-progress are measured by using the first-in first-out (FIFO) or weighted-average cost method. The cost comprises costs of purchase and other direct costs incurred. Taxpayers may continue to include the indirect costs (Art. 29 CCCTB-PCD). The acquisition of assets is recorded in an asset register (Art. 32 CCCTB-PCD). Assets are depreciated on the basis of the cost directly connected with the acquisition of a fixed asset. If fixed assets are made by the company, the indirect costs incurred in production of the asset are to be added to the depreciation base (Art. 33 CCCTB-PCD).

These rules reflect the principles forming the basis of tax accounting in the Member States: net principle, realization principle, historical cost accounting and separate valuation of assets and liabilities. Major conceptual deviations from current tax accounting practice of the Member States pertain to recognition and measurement of provisions.[37]

---

[37] See Spengel/Zöllkau (2012).

Consolidation of Profits

Each member of a CCCTB-group separately determines its profits according to the harmonized tax accounting rules. The profits and losses of all group members are pooled and profits and losses from intra-group transactions are eliminated. In order to prevent the group's profit from being subject to economic double taxation, taxable profit is realized when goods are sold or services are provided by group members to third parties (Art. 59 CCCTB-PCD). Intra-group dividends are tax-free.

Regarding the consolidation techniques common consolidation rules could be followed. In financial accounting, the purchase method (IFRS 3.14) is used for consolidation. The affiliate's net assets replace the parent's shareholdings in the consolidated accounts. If the book value of the shareholding exceeds the book value of net assets, there is a step-up in the book value of assets (including a goodwill) in the consolidated accounts. However, this step-up is a questionable element of the tax accounting rules applicable under CCCTB. If, in the course of consolidation, corporations benefit from a tax-free step-up, the step-up saves future taxes because future profits are reduced by the higher book values of the assets used or sold. Hidden reserves could escape the corporation tax. From this perspective, a step-up upon consolidation must trigger taxes. In order to avoid tax payments upon consolidation, tax consolidation rules must be based on book values and carry over hidden reserves from the tax base of single companies to the common tax base of the group.

As a result of consolidation, profits and losses from different countries are mutually offset. If the EU-wide operations of a group are successful overall, there should be sufficient profits to absorb the losses. Then interest and cash flow disadvantages from the deferred offset of losses vanish. Each Member State shares in group member's loss in proportion to its share in the overall profit or loss. If there is an overall loss, a carry-forward is foreseen (Art. 43 CCCTB-PCD).

5.2.2. Formula Apportionment

The group's profit is allocated to the Member States where the group has taxable activities under a common formula. The definition of the formula's factors and the specification of their weight is one of the key problems of CCCTB. All participating Member States will have to agree upon the formula in order to avoid overlapping tax bases or tax base loopholes.

The design of a formula cannot be justified solely on the grounds of economic reasoning. It is impossible to determine the amount of profit caused by any given factor of the formula. To determine the factors and their weight is a political decision to be taken in the light of the economic effects of the formula. In the first place, Member States will aim at a fair allocation of corporation tax revenues. In the second place, the formula must aim at simplicity and legal certainty in order to reduce compliance costs as well as administrative costs of formula apportionment. In the third place, the formula should be resistant against tax planning of European groups. An agreement may be difficult to reach because Member States will be aware that the formula directly impacts on their corporation tax revenue.

Factors of the Formula

In general, microeconomic factors, such as capital, wages, sales and value added, or macroeconomic factors, such as the gross domestic product and per capita national income of a Member State, can be used to apportion the profit of a CCCTB-group among Member States. Macroeconomic factors allocate the profit according to a Member State's share in, for example, the gross domestic product of all Member States where the group has taxable activities. Macroeconomic factors obviously have the advantage of a comparatively high robustness against manipulation by tax planning. On the other hand, profits are apportioned without reference to the scope and type of a group's economic activities in each Member State. Small Member States may lose tax revenue because of their smaller size in comparison to larger countries.

Microeconomic factors have the advantage of being based on the economic characteristics of the group. Production factors such as capital and labor reflect the internationally established right of the source country to tax profits of local origin. However, according to internationally established source rules, sales do not form a basis for a country's tax claim on profits. Nevertheless, sales may be justified as a part of the apportionment formula, when they relate to the marketing activities of a group in a Member State. Sales may reward a Member State for providing a market infrastructure to the group. Value added as a factor could take advantage of the already harmonized tax base of the value added tax in the EU. Yet, if value added is determined by deducting payments to other group companies from sales, transfer pricing issues are reintroduced through the backdoor.

An agreement regarding the factors of the formula is necessary, but not sufficient. Member States have also to agree on the appropriate weighting of the factors. Given a three-factor formula with capital, labor and sales, Member States with manufacturing facilities will be in favor of a higher weighting on capital and wages. Member States where goods are sold will be in favor of a higher weighting on sales. Reaching an agreement on a common apportionment formula will definitely not be an easy task.

The European Commission's Formula

The European Commission proposes a three-factor formula, based on capital, labor and sales (Art. 86 CCCTB-PCD). The factor labor includes the number of employees and the payroll (Art. 90 CCCTB-PCD). The tax liability in a Member State is determined as

$$
\begin{aligned}
T_{MS} &= \tau_{MS} \cdot \pi \cdot \left[\alpha_{MS}^{C} \cdot \frac{C_{MS}}{C} + \alpha_{MS}^{L} \cdot \left(\beta_1 \cdot \frac{L_{MS}}{L} + \beta_2 \cdot \frac{N_{MS}}{N}\right) + \alpha_{MS}^{S} \cdot \frac{S_{MS}}{S}\right] \\
&= \tau_{MS} \cdot \pi \cdot F_{MS}
\end{aligned} \tag{5.1}
$$

with T_{MS}: tax liability in Member State MS; τ_{MS}: statutory tax rate in Member State MS; π: overall group profit; C_{MS}: capital in Member State MS; L_{MS}: wages in Member State MS; N_{MS}: number of employees in Member State MS; S_{MS}: sales in Member State MS; C: overall group capital; L: overall group wages; N: overall number of employees; S: overall group sales; α_{MS}*: factor of weight for capital, wages and sales with $\Sigma\ \alpha_{MS}^* = 1$; β_k: factor of weight for payroll and employees with $\Sigma\ \beta_k = 1$; F_{MS}: total share of Member States MS with $\sum F_{MS} = 1$.

According to the European Commission's proposal, the factor weighting for capital, labor and sales equal $\alpha_{MS}^* = 1/3$ and the β-factors are $\beta_k = 1/2$.

The factor capital includes all fixed tangible assets owned, rented or leased, valued at historical cost. Intangible assets are partly included by a rule that captures the total amount of costs incurred for research, development, marketing and advertising over the six years that preceded the first application of the formula (Art. 92-94 CCCTB-PCD). Employees and payroll are included in the labor factor of the group member which pays the wages. Sales are defined as proceeds of all sales of goods and supplies of services to third parties net of taxes. Sales are allocated to group members on a destination basis. Sales enter the sales factor of the group member where dispatch or transport of the goods ends. Services are included in the sales factor of the group member where the services are carried out (Art. 95 and Art. 96 CCCTB-PCD).

The consolidated tax base is only shared in case of an overall profit. Losses are allowed to be deducted from profits in subsequent years. The oldest losses have to be used first (Art. 86 CCCTB-PCD).

The average tax rate of the group τ_G with taxable activities in n Member States is determined by the Member States' statutory tax rates τ_{MS} and the Member States' total share F_{MS} according to the apportionment formula:

(5.2) $$\tau_G = \sum_{MS=1}^{n} \tau_{MS} \cdot F_{MS}$$

According to equation (5.2), the profits tax becomes a tax on the factors included into the formula.

Example (5.2): G Corporation, located in Member State G, owns 100% of the shareholdings in A Corporation, resident in Member State A. The following table displays G&A group's capital, payroll, number of employees, sales and profit (determined according to the common tax accounting rules, numbers in thousands).

	G Corporation	A Corporation	G&A Group
Capital	25,000	5,000	30,000
Payroll	3,000	1,500	4,500
Employees	40	10	50
Sales	30,000	6,000	36,000
Profit			4,500

G&A group´s profit is attributed to the Member States G and A respectively according to the formula proposed by the European Commission. The table displays the elements of the formula, the attributed share of total profit and the tax payments in both Member States.

	G Corporation	A Corporation	G&A Group
Share in capital	0.83	0.17	1.00
Share in payroll	0.67	0.33	1.00
Share in number of employees	0.80	0.20	1.00
Share in sales	0.83	0.17	1.00
Total share at equal weights	0.80	0.20	1.00
Share in total profit	3,600	900	4,500
Corporation tax rate	0.30	0.20	
Corporation tax	1,080	180	1,260
Average tax rate			28%

The formula allocates 20% of the group´s profit to Member State A where it is taxed at a rate of 20%. A share of 80% of the group´s profit is allocated to Member State G where it is taxed at a rate of 30%. The group´s corporation tax payment amounts to 1,260 with an average tax rate of 28% (= 1,260/4,500).

Under the European Commission's three-factor formula, the average tax rate of the CCCTB group approaches the corporation tax rate of the Member State where to group has located the majority of its business functions in terms of capital, labor and sales.

Tax Planning

Although the CCCTB eliminates profit shifting opportunities provided by applicable law under the OECD approach, it offers new tax planning opportunities. Formulae based on microeconomic factors are vulnerable to tax planning. The tax bill increases in the country where one of the factors increases.

Whereas under the current separate entity approach of the OECD, book profits as well as real investments can be shifted, tax planning under formula apportionment focuses exclusively on the location of real investments. European groups experience an incentive to transfer business functions and assets captured by the formula to low-tax Member States. The transfer of business functions is greatly facilitated because it does not trigger exit taxes. All profits from intra-group transactions are eliminated by means of consolidation. The group's average tax rate is reduced if the group increases capital, wages, employees or sales in a low-tax Member State at the expense of the same factors in a high-tax Member State.

Example (5.3): G&A group Example (5.2) transfers business functions to the low-tax Member State A resulting in a reduction of capital invested, payroll, number of employees and sales in Member State G. The group´s total profit is assumed to remain unaffected in order to isolate the pure tax planning effect. The following tables display the effects on the groups accounting and tax data.

	G Corporation	A Corporation	G&A Group
Capital	5,000	25,000	30,000
Payroll	1,500	3,000	4,500
Employees	10	40	50
Sales	6,000	30,000	36,000
Profit			4,500

	G Corporation	A Corporation	G&A Group
Share in capital	0.17	0.83	1.00
Share in payroll	0.33	0.67	1.00
Share in number of employees	0.20	0.80	1.00
Share in sales	0.17	0.83	1.00
Total share at equal weights	0.20	0.80	1.00
Share in total profit	900	3,600	20.00
Corporation tax rate	0.30	0.20	
Corporation tax	270	720	990
Average tax rate			22%

After the transfer of business functions to Member State A, the formula allocates 80% of the group´s profit to Member State A and 20% to Member State G. The group´s corporation tax payments amount to 990 resulting in an average tax rate of 22% (= 990/4,500). The transfer of business functions reduces the average tax rate by six percentage points.

Because formula apportionment works like a tax on each variable, tax planning incentives differ with the design of the formula. A formula based on both production and sales is more resistant against the transfer of business functions than, e.g., a formula which takes only production functions into account. Yet, each single factor can be influenced with tax planning.

Once CCCTB is implemented, corporation tax rates will be the driving tax factors for investment decisions within the EU because differences in the tax base determination vanish. Member States will experience an increased pressure on their statutory corporation tax rates. High rates can no longer be compensated by favorable tax accounting rules. Profit shifting through transfer prices and debt financing, which to certain extent can cushion high statutory tax rates, is impossible within a CCCTB group. Due to the common tax base, the tax burden the companies face in a Member State is more transparent. As a result, tax competition among Member States of the EU is intensified with respect to the statutory corporation tax rate.

Safeguard Clause and Anti-Abuse Rules

The European Commission proposes a safeguard clause that gives the taxpayer and the taxing authority the right to request the use of an alternative method (Art. 87 CCCTB-PCD). The safeguard clause is targeted at cases where the outcome of formula apportionment has to be considered as an unfair profit allocation. However, all taxing authorities involved have to agree to the alternative method. This condition significantly reduces the application of the safeguard clause.

The European Commission proposes an asset relocation rule. As an anti-abuse rule the asset relocation rule is targeted at the transfer of business functions. In case of an asset transfer within the group, all assets transferred have to be included into the factor capital of the transferring company for the five years following the transfer (Art. 70 CCCTB-PCD). The asset relocation rule may serve as a brake on the tax driven transfer of manufacturing. However, the group may also redirect sales to low-tax Member States. Although the redirection of sales to private customers will be virtually impossible, a sales redirection to business customers may be facilitated, because they are more mobile in terms of place of acquisition.

5.3. Entering and Leaving the Group

5.3.1. Transfer of Assets

A group exercising the option for the CCCTB transfers its business assets to the common tax base. This may be accomplished at book value. With a book value transfer, hidden reserves are transferred from a Member States' tax base to the common tax base. Upon the transfer of assets to the common tax base, the Member States where the group has taxable activities acquire a tax claim to the hidden reserves transferred according to the formula, whereas the tax claim of the country where the hidden reserves accrued is reduced to its share of profit under the formula. In effect, the book value transfer erodes a Member State's tax claim on hidden reserves transferred.

Book value transfer offers European groups tax planning opportunities. In principle, hidden reserves can be transferred from a high-tax Member State to low-tax Member States without triggering taxes. Thus, a European group may be able to choose where to pay taxes on an asset's hidden reserves. More specifically, a European group faces the choice of selling an asset outside or inside the group. If the asset is sold outside the group, the profit will be taxed at the corporation tax rate of the selling corporation. If the asset is transferred to the common tax base and sold after the transfer, the profit is taxed at the average tax rate of the group. A group performing its business functions in low-tax Member States may face an average tax rate which is well below the rate of the high-tax Member State.

Exit Taxation

To restrict tax planning opportunities, hidden reserves accrued in a Member State can be immediately taxed by this Member State when the hidden reserves are transferred to the common tax base (exit taxation). Exit taxes are levied on the difference between market value and tax book value of assets at the time of exit. Assets are to be transferred to the common tax base at their market value to avoid economic double taxation of the hidden reserves. If a corporation leaves the CCCTB group (e.g. because the shareholding requirements are no longer met or because the corporation is merged into a corporation which does not belong to the CCCTB group), the hidden reserves of the assets leaving the common tax base have to be assessed and have to be apportioned to the CCCTB Member States according to the formula in order to uphold the taxing rights of the Member States involved.

Exit taxation is unavoidable if Member States are not willing to forego their tax claim to hidden reserves which accrued under their jurisdiction. On the other hand, exit taxes may render the CCCTB regime unattractive for European groups. Exit taxes are levied on all assets of a company including self-generated goodwill. The goodwill of a corporation transferring its assets to the common tax base would be taxed immediately. In effect, exit taxes would be charged on the difference of the equity's market value and its book value. Thus, the amount of exit taxes could be very high.

The European Commission's Proposal

Under the rules proposed by the European Commission a group opting for CCCTB will form the group at book value. With respect to assets entering and leaving the group, strict exit taxation is not prescribed. However, special rules aim at preventing abuse when assets are transferred to or from the common tax base.

If assets are disposed of by a group member within five years after the asset's date of entry into the group, an adjustment is made. The gain from the disposal (proceeds of the disposal less tax book value of the asset sold) is added to the share of the group's profit allocated to the Member State to which the asset belonged before entry into the group (Art. 61 CCCTB-PCD).

If assets are disposed of by a company which has left the group within three years preceding the assets' disposal, the gain from the disposal (proceeds of the disposal less tax book value of the asset sold) is added to the consolidated tax base (Art. 67 CCCTB-PCD). If a company leaves the group which is the owner of self-generated intangible assets, the cost incurred (and deducted from the consolidated tax base) has to be added back to the consolidated tax base. The amount added back is limited to the market value of the intangible assets. The amount added back is attributed to the leaving company where it may be deducted according to applicable tax law (Art. 68 CCCTB-PCD).

In principle, the European Commission's proposal eliminates exit taxation when a group opts for the CCCTB. However, the proposed rules include anti-abuse provisions to hinder tax planning. However, the time component of the rules may weaken their effect. Apart from this, they may prove to be too general and thus infringe primary European law.

5.3.2. Transfer of Shares

Corporations usually do not pay taxes on gains from the sale of shares. Under the European Commission's proposal the same rules will apply to the common tax base (Art. 11 CCCTB-PCD). Each CCCTB group company will be able to sell shareholdings tax-free. In principle, the tax exemption of capital gains is necessary to avoid double taxation of profits at the hands of a corporation. Without tax exemption of capital gains, profits of a group company would be taxed twice: initially when the profits accrue and subsequently when the capital gain is realized.

Tax Planning Opportunities

Nonetheless, the exemption of capital gains from the tax base is an incentive to combine the tax-free transfer of assets within the CCCTB group with a subsequent tax free share deal. In effect, a taxable asset deal could be transformed into a tax-free share deal. A corporation belonging to a CCCTB group may be able to transfer an asset to a non-CCCTB group corporation at book value avoiding taxes on the accrued hidden reserves.

Example (5.4): G Corporation owns a valuable intangible asset with a tax book value of zero. The corporate shareholder sells its shareholding in G Corporation tax-free to F Corporation which belongs to a CCCTB-group. G Corporation becomes a member of the CCCTB group. G Corporation transfers the intangible asset tax-free to I Corporation, another CCCTB group member wholly owned by F Corporation. After the asset transfer, F Corporation sells the shares in I Corporation tax-free to P Corporation, a non-CCCTB corporation. After the transaction, I Corporation sells the intangible asset to a third party and realizes the hidden reserves. Upon realization, the hidden reserves are burdened with corporation taxes of the Member State where I Corporation is resident. As a result of this sequence of transactions, the hidden reserves are transferred tax-free from Member State G to Member State I.

By interposing a CCCTB group company and combining asset deals and share deals, corporations will be able to engage in international tax rate arbitrage by shifting the tax base from one country to another. Such a loophole will have to be closed.

Anti-Abuse Rule

The European Commission proposes an anti-abuse rule which is triggered if the sale of the shares and the transfer of the asset both take place within a certain period of time. If a corporation leaves the CCCTB group through a tax-free share deal and the same corporation has acquired an asset in an intra-group transaction within the current or previous year, an amount corresponding to the hidden reserves attaching to the asset is excluded from the tax exemption of the share deal. This rule is waived if there are sound business reasons for the transaction. The amount excluded from exemption is defined as the difference between the asset's market value and the asset's tax book value (Art. 75 CCCTB-PCD).

As yet, it is unclear whether this rule will be effective in practice. The waiver for transactions for sound business reasons may open a loophole for the transfer tax planner.

5.3.3. Business Reorganizations

The Mergers Directive allows a Member State to tax the hidden reserves of assets leaving its jurisdiction upon merger (e.g. if a German corporation is merged onto a French corporation). Under the applicable law, a cross-border merger may trigger a substantial amount of corporation taxes. Should the same rules apply to mergers within a CCCTB group? On the one hand, transfers of assets within a CCCTB group are not taxed. Only profits stemming from transactions with third parties are subject to formula allocation and subsequent taxation. On the other hand, the tax-free transfer of hidden reserves deprives the Member State of accrual of the right to tax the respective profits.

According to the European Commission's proposal, business reorganizations within a CCCTB-group do not give rise to profit or loss and thus are not taxable events (Art. 70 CCCTB-PCD). One may argue that a tax-free transfer of hidden reserves on the occasion of business reorganizations can be accepted by Member States, because they participate in future profits upon the realization of the hidden reserves in proportion to their share in the overall profit. As against this, the effect may be that a Member State exchanges a substantial tax claim of its own for an insignificantly small part of the whole if the group has ceased to perform substantial economic activities there when the hidden reserves are realized.

European groups have an incentive to engage in international tax arbitrage. In the course of business reorganization, the assets of a group company may be transferred to another Member State thereby changing the capital factor of the apportionment formula. If the capital factor in a low-tax Member States increases, the group's tax base is shifted to that low-tax Member State. As a result, business reorganizations may be used to reduce the group's average tax rate.

Anti-Abuse Rule

An anti-abuse rule deals with losses in tax revenue in cases where, as a result of business reorganization, substantially all the assets of a group member are transferred to another Member State within a period of two years. In such cases, the assets transferred are attributed to the asset factor of the transferring company throughout the next five years (Art. 70 CCCTB-PCD). This increases the share in the group's profit allocated to the Member State of origin and delays the fall in the average tax rate of the group.

European groups' international tax planning may not be effectively curbed by an anti-abuse rule which only indirectly addresses transferred hidden reserves. In fiscal terms, immediate exit taxation of hidden reserves and deferred taxation of hidden reserves transferred through an increased share in the group´s profit due to a temporally higher capital factor are not the same.

In sum, the taxation of hidden reserves seems to be a weakness of the CCCTB. Given the corporation tax rate differentials in the EU, the tax planning incentives are high. Transfer tax planning endangers the tax revenue of Member States with comparatively high corporation tax rates. On the other hand, the common consolidated tax base may not be very attractive to European companies if the transfer of hidden reserves is immediately taxed.

5.4. Non-EU Countries

The scope of the CCCTB is limited to the European Union (water's edge restriction). However, European corporation tax harmonization goes far beyond a common corporate tax base and a common apportionment formula for a European CCCTB-group´s profits. Common rules with respect to transactions of CCCTB-group members with non-EU group members are also needed.

Tax planning incentives caused by separate entity accounting are still there with respect to non-EU countries. A Europe based multinational group may thus follow a dual set of tax planning strategies. Within the European Union, the planning is targeted at the apportionment formula, whereas outside the European Union the well-known tax planning instruments under the separate entity approach are still available. Multinationals have an incentive to shift profits and investments to a non-EU country if the CCCTB group's average tax rate is higher than the tax rate in the non-EU country. There is still a need for the Member States to cope with this traditional type of international tax planning.

If a Member State effectively combats international profit shifting to countries outside the EU, this Member State increases the common tax base. The tax revenues of the respective Member State, on the other hand, are only increased to the extent that the formula allocates the additional profits to this Member State. A Member State which is less restrictive with respect to profit shifting from the common tax base to non-EU countries decreases the common tax base at the expense of other Member States. Under these circumstances, Member States may not feel a strong incentive to restrict international profit shifting.

A Member State reluctant to prevent profit shifting, may become more attractive as a location for European groups. A CCCTB group might use companies located in this Member State to shift profits outside the EU. As a result, the common tax base shrinks. All Member States suffer from the loss in tax revenue, exempt for the Member State of the group, which enjoys an increase in its own corporation tax revenue. Common anti-abuse rules dealing with non-EU countries are necessary to avoid these negative effects on the common tax base.

Debt Financing

A company belonging to a CCCTB-group can be financed with debt by a group company resident in a non-EU country. The CCCTB group deducts interest expenses from the common tax base, whereas the corresponding interest income is taxed in a non-EU country. To avoid international tax planning by means of internal debt and to protect the common tax base, the European Commission proposes rules to disallow the deduction of interest payments to associated companies resident in a non-EU country under certain conditions.

Interest payments on internal debt are not tax-deductible if there is no agreement on information exchange with the non-EU country and if the corporation tax rate in the non-EU country is lower than 40% of the average statutory tax rate in the Member States, or if the non-EU country offers a special tax regime with a level of taxation which is substantially lower than that of the common tax regime. Moreover, the interest payment has to conform to the arm´s length standard and interest payments are only tax-deductible if the corresponding interest income is part of the foreign tax base (Art. 81 CCCTB-PCD).

The rules targeted at excessive internal debt financing may prove to be not very effective. Most countries comply with information exchange requirements and because the average corporation tax rate in the EU amounts to 23.80% (as of 2011), the foreign corporation tax rate must be lower than 9.52% (= 40% · 23.80%). A tax rate differential of 14.28% (= 23.80 – 9.52%) may be attractive enough to engage in debt financing via internal loans granted to group companies located in non-EU countries.

Controlled Foreign Companies

Foreign corporations continue to shelter income from shareholder taxation if the respective corporations are located in non-EU countries. A CCCTB-group thus may shift profits from the common tax base to a non-EU company. The European Commission's proposal contains CFC rules targeted at subsidiaries in non-EU countries (Art. 82 CCCTB-PCD). Retained profits of a non-EU subsidiary are included in the common tax base if the following conditions are fulfilled: (i) the shareholding exceeds 50%, (ii) the foreign statutory corporation tax rate is lower than 40% of the average statutory tax rate applicable in the Member States, (iii) more than 30% of the foreign income is not derived from active trading (e.g. interest income, dividends, royalties) and (iv) the company´s shares are not regularly traded. Profits previously included in the tax base under these above rules are excluded from the tax base if the foreign corporation distributes them (Art. 83 CCCTB-PCD).

If a foreign dividend is only lightly taxed, a switch over clause allows a Member State to switch over from the exemption method (prescribed in Art. 11 CCCTB-PCD) to the credit method of avoiding double taxation. Switch over is possible, if the corporation which made the profit distribution is resident in a non-EU country and subject to a statutory corporation tax rate which is lower than 40% of the average EU statutory corporation tax rate (Art.73 CCCTB-PCD).

Both CFC rules and switch over clause might not be tight enough, because foreign tax rates above 40% of the average EU corporation tax rate leave a CCCTB group enough room for maneuver.

Transfer Prices

Profits from intra-group transactions are taxed and transfer prices have to be established for tax purposes if companies are involved which do not belong to the CCCTB group. EU corporations belonging to a CCCTB group with subsidiaries or permanent establishments in non-EU countries face a dual tax system. Within the CCCTB group, profits are allocated according to formula apportionment. Outside the CCCTB group, the established OECD transfer pricing rules apply. With respect to non-EU countries, all Member States must apply the OECD transfer pricing rules in the same way.

Given the vagueness of the OECD rules in cases where firm-specific assets are transferred or firm-specific services are provided to or from non-EU companies, it is not ensured that Member States will apply the transfer pricing rules in same way. Again, Member States may be tempted to grant some room for maneuver to European groups in order to attract business and to increase their share in in the common tax base. European groups may have a preference for certain Member States when performing transactions with non-EU group companies.

Reading List Chapter 5

Agúendez-Garcia, Ana: The Delineation and Apportionment of an EU Consolidated Tax Base for Multi-Jurisdictual Corporate Income Taxation, European Commission Working Paper No. 9, 2006.

Avi-Yonah, Reuven S.; Benshalom, Ilan: Formulary Apportionment – Myths and Prospects. Promoting Better International Tax Policies by Utilizing the Misunderstood and Under-Theorized Formulary Alternative, in: World Tax Journal 2011, pp. 371-398.

Cnossen, Sijbren (ed.): Taxing Capital Income in the European Union: Issues and Options for Reform, Oxford, 2000.

Devereux, Michael P.: Debating Proposed Reforms of the Taxation of Corporate Income in the European Union, in: International Tax and Public Finance, 2004, pp. 71-89.

European Commission: Proposal for a Council Directive on a Common Consolidated Corporate Tax Base (CCCTB), COM (2011) 212/4, Brussels, 2011.

European Commission: European Tax Survey, Working Paper 3/2004, Office for Official Publications of the European Communities, Luxembourg, 2004.

European Commission: Company Taxation in the Internal Market, Commission Staff Working paper, Luxembourg, 2002.

Fuest, Clemens; Hemmelgarn, Thomas; Ramb, Fred: How Would the Introduction of an EU-wide Formula Apportionment Affect the Distribution and Size of the Corporate Tax Base? An Analysis Based on German Multinationals, in: International Tax and Public Finance 2007, pp. 627-648.

Gammie, Malcolm; Giannini, Silvia; Klemm, Alexander; Oestreicher, Andreas; Parancandolo, Paola; Spengel, Christoph: Achieving a Common Consolidated Corporate Tax Base in the EU, 2006.

Hellerstein, Jerome R.; Hellerstein, Walter: State Taxation, 3rd Edition, Boston, 2007.

Hellerstein, Walter; McLure, Charles E. Jr.: The European Commission's Report on Company Income Taxation: What the EU can Learn from the Experience of the US States, in: International Tax and Public Finance 2004, pp. 199-220.

Lang, Michael; Pistone, Pasquale; Schuch, Josef; Staringer, Claus: Common Consolidated Corporate Tax Base, Vienna, 2008.

Martens-Weiner, Joann: Company Tax Reform in the European Union. Guidance from the United States and Canada on Implementing Formulary Apportionment in the EU, New York, 2006.

McLure, Charles E. Jr.: Corporate Tax Harmonization in the European Union: The Commission's Proposals, in: Tax Notes International 2004, pp. 775–801.

Miller, Angharad; Oats, Lynne: Principles of International Taxation, West Sussex, 2009.

Mintz, Jack: Corporate Tax Harmonization in Europe: It's All About Compliance, in: International Tax and Public Finance 2004, pp. 221-234.

Munin, Nellie: Tax in Troubled Time: Is it the Time for a Common Consolidated Corporate Tax Base in the EU, in: EC Tax Review 2011, pp. 121-133.

Oestreicher, Andreas; Reister, Timo; Spengel, Christoph: Common Corporate Tax Base and Effective Tax Burdens in the EU Member States, in: World Tax Journal 2009, pp. 44-66.

Schön, Wolfgang; Schreiber, Ulrich; Spengel, Christoph: A Common Consolidated Corporate Tax Base for Europe, Heidelberg, 2008.

Schreiber, Ulrich: The Taxation of Hidden Reserves under the Common Consolidated Corporate Tax Base, in: European Taxation 2009, pp.84-91.

Sørensen, Peter Birch: Company Tax Reform in the European Union, in: International Tax and Public Finance, Vol. 11, 2004, pp. 91-115.

Spengel, Christoph; Zöllkau, York: Common Corporate Tax Base (CC(C)TB) and Determination of Taxable Income. An International Comparison, Heidelberg, 2012.

6. International Tax Planning and Accounting for Income Taxes

6.1. The Role of Income Tax Reporting

Listed European corporations have to comply with international accounting standards. These companies draw up their accounts according to endorsed International Financial Reporting Standards (IFRS). IFRS are designed to provide useful information to present and potential investors, lenders and other creditors, who use that information to make financial decisions. As taxes reduce the profit available for distribution to shareholders, the effective tax burden must be disclosed.

Tax Accounting versus Financial Accounting

Tax accounting and financial accounting very often diverge. This is obviously the case in countries operating a two-book system which strictly separates tax accounting and financial accounting. Even in countries with a one-book system where, in principle, tax accounting conforms to financial accounting, divergences between the two are common.

Taxable profits and profits in financial accounts are often determined differently. Tax expenses based on taxable profits may not properly relate to profits reported in the financial accounts. IAS 12 is thus targeted at synchronizing tax expenses and accounting profits in order to provide meaningful information on the effective tax burden. Companies account for the tax consequences of transactions in the same way as they account for the transactions themselves. IAS 12 deals with income taxes, including withholding taxes. Other taxes, such as value added taxes, are not covered by the standard.

Tax Planning

Because income tax reporting serves the objective of providing useful information to a company's shareholders and creditors, companies have to disclose detailed information on the relation of reported tax expense to the pre-tax accounting profit (the effective tax rate). Capital markets monitor the effective tax rate and evaluate the effect of a company's tax planning on its profitability.

Successful tax planning strategies positively impact on a company's net profit and the effective tax rate. In fact, a company may find that a comparatively small amount of tax savings has the same effect on net profits as a considerable increase in sales.

Example (6.1): M Corporation reports sales of € 60,000,000, profit before taxes of € 6,000,000, and corporation taxes of € 2,400,000 €, resulting in an after-tax profit of € 3,600,000. The operating profit margin and the effective tax rate are 10% (= 6/60) and 40% (= 2.4/6.0) respectively. M Corporation implements a tax planning strategy reducing income tax expenses by € 360,000 to € 2,040,000. The effective tax rate is reduced by 6 percentage points from 40% to 34% (= 2.04/6.0). As a result, the after-tax profit increases by 10% to 3,960,000 (= 6,000,000 – 2,040,000). To achieve the same result, M corporation would have to increase sales by € 6,000,000. Given the operating profit margin of 10%, the profit before taxes is then increased by € 600,000 to € 6,600,000, triggering € 2,640,000 (= 40% · 6,600,000) in corporation tax and resulting in an after-tax profit of € 3,960,000.

Given the strong effects of successful tax planning on a company's accounting profit and given the relevance of accounting profits for the market value of the company, the effective tax rate is an important driver of a publicly owned company's market value. Thus, the effective tax rate influences both corporate tax planning strategies and shareholders' investment decisions.[38]

6.2. The Effective Tax Rate

6.2.1. Cash Flow Based Effective Tax Rate

A company's market value is determined by after-tax cash flows and the market rate of return. As a consequence, tax planning focuses on the after-tax cash flow and on the after-tax NPV. In order to calculate the effective tax rate (*ETR*), the company's tax burden in present value terms (*NPVT*) has to be related to its pre-tax economic profit in present value terms (*NPVP*). More formally, the *ETR* can be defined as the ratio of the NPV of taxes at time $t = 0$ and the NPV of economic profits at time $t = 0$:

$$ETR = \frac{NPVT_0}{NPVP_0}. \quad (6.1)$$

From this economic perspective, the *ETR* does not depend on accounting figures but on cash flows in present value terms.

[38] See Scholes et al., 2009, pp. 44.

Economic Profit

The starting point for the determination of economic profit is the NPV of the investments' pre-tax cash flows. The NPV of a company's pre-tax cash flows at time t, discounted at the market interest rate i, amounts to

(6.2) $$PV_t = \sum_{z=t+1}^{n} CF_z \cdot (1+i)^{-(z-t)} .$$

Economic depreciation at time t is indicated by the investments' decline (or increase) in value:

(6.3) $$ED_t = PV_{t-1} - PV_t .$$

The pre-tax economic profit at time t is the difference between cash flow and economic depreciation:

(6.4) $$EP_t = CF_t - ED_t .$$

The economic profit at time t equals the pre-tax market return on the investments' pre-tax NPV, i.e. the product of the market interest rate i and the pre-tax NPV of the investment at time $t-1$:[39]

(6.5) $$EP_t = i \cdot PV_{t-1}.$$

The economic profit is the periodic market return on the present value of the investment's cash flows. As opposed to economic profit, accounting profit is essentially based on historical costs of assets and liabilities which are individually recognized and valued.

Income Taxes

Income taxes are levied on taxable profit as the tax base. Taxable profit is determined on the basis of accrual accounting. If the investment outlay is capitalized under tax accounting rules, subsequent cash flows are reduced by the amount of depreciation. Ignoring other accruals, taxable profit at time t amounts to

(6.6) $$TP_t = CF_t - D_t$$

[39] See Samuelson (1964).

with D_t denoting depreciation for tax purposes. Formally, equation (6.6) has the same structure as equation (6.4). Yet, economic depreciation (ED_t) depends on future cash flows, whereas tax depreciation (D_t) is determined by the investment outlay (historical acquisition cost).

The NPV of taxes paid at time $t = 0$, discounted at the after-tax market interest rate i_τ, is

(6.7) $$NPVT_0 = \sum_{t=1}^{n} \tau_{RI} \cdot TP_t \cdot (1 + i_\tau)^{-t}$$

with τ_{RI} indicating the statutory tax rate. The NPV of the economic profit at time $t = 0$ is defined as the difference between cash flow and economic depreciation, discounted at the after-tax market interest rate:

(6.8) $$NPVP_0 = \sum_{t=1}^{n} EP_t \cdot (1 + i_\tau)^{-t} .$$

Taxes as well as economic profits are discounted at the after-tax market interest rate as business profits and interest income are generally subject to tax.

Economic Profit versus Taxable Profit

Taxable profit equals economic profit if tax depreciation equals economic depreciation ($D_t = ED_t$). Then, the tax base does not influence the *ETR*. Given a uniform statutory tax rate, the investments' effective tax rate equals the statutory tax rate ($ETR = \tau_{RI}$). If tax depreciation differs from economic depreciation, the tax base is no longer neutral with respect to the *ETR*. The *ETR* may be greater than the statutory tax rate ($ETR > \tau_{RI}$), indicating that the tax base disadvantages the investment, or lower than the statutory tax rate ($ETR < \tau_{RI}$), indicating that the tax base favors the investment.

If, for example, an asset is not recognized in the tax account, the investment outlay being fully expensed for tax purposes, its tax book value is zero and future cash flows are fully taxed. Both the investment outlay and the proceeds from the investment are reduced by taxes. The company faces a tax charged on cash flow rather than on profit. The *ETR* falls short of the statutory corporation tax rate, indicating that the tax base favors the investment.

Example (6.2): A company invests 1,000 and faces a corporation tax rate $\tau_{RI} = 40\%$. The investment outlay is capitalized for tax purposes and depreciated. The market interest rate amounts to $i = 10\%$. The after-tax interest rate amounts to $i_\tau = 6\%$.

t	0	1	2	3
I_0	-1,000,00			
CF_t		600.00	300.00	275.00
PV_t	1,000.00	500.00	250.00	0.00
$i \cdot PV_{t-1}$		100.00	50.00	25.00
D_t		500.00	250.00	250.00
$CF_t - D_t$		100.00	50.00	25.00
T_t		40.00	20.00	10.00
$I_0 + CF_t - T_t$	-1000.00	560.00	280.00	265.00
NPV after taxes	$C_0^\tau = -1{,}000 + \frac{560}{1.06} + \frac{280}{1.06^2} + \frac{265}{1.06^3} = 0$			
$NPVT_0$	$63.93 = \frac{40}{1.06} + \frac{20}{1.06^2} + \frac{10}{1.06^3}$			
$NPVP_0$	$159.83 = \frac{100}{1.06} + \frac{50}{1.06^2} + \frac{25}{1.06^3}$			
ETR	40%			

Depreciation for tax purposes equals economic depreciation (the decline in value of the cash flows). As a result, the tax base equals economic profit. The effective tax rate amounts to $ETR = 40\%$ indicating that the tax base does not influence the tax burden on the profits generated by the investment.

If the asset is immediately expensed, the investor receives a tax refund at time $t = 0$ and is fully taxed on the investment's cash flows at time $t > 0$.

t	0	1	2	3
I_0	-1,000,00			
CF_t		600.00	300.00	275.00
PV_t	1,000.00	500.00	250.00	0.00
$i \cdot PV_{t-1}$		100.00	50.00	25.00
D_t	1,000.00	0.00	0.00	0.00
$CF_t - D_t$	-1,000.00	600.00	300.00	275.00
T_t	-400.00	240.00	120.00	110.00
$I_0 + CF_t - T_t$	-600.00	360.00	180.00	165.00
NPV after taxes	$C_0^T = -600 + \frac{360}{1.06} + \frac{180}{1.06^2} + \frac{165}{1.06^3} = 38{,}36$			
$NPVT_0$	$25.57 = -400 + \frac{240}{1.06} + \frac{120}{1.06^2} + \frac{110}{1.06^3}$			
$NPVI_0$	$159.83 = \frac{100}{1.06} + \frac{50}{1.06^2} + \frac{25}{1.06^3}$			
ETR	16%			

Expensing the investment outlay at time $t = 0$ generates a tax refund of 400.00. The NPV of taxes paid is reduced to 25.57 and consequently the investment's NPV increases whereas the effective tax rate drops to 16%. The *ETR* falls short of the statutory tax rate indicating that the tax base favors the investment.

In effect, the cash flow based *ETR* relates the NPV of taxes to the NPV of economic profits. The *ETR* correctly measures the effective tax burden and accurately shows the financial effects of tax planning.

6.2.2. Accounting Based Effective Tax Rate

Accrual accounting builds on transactions and transforms net cash flow to profits and losses by allocating cash flows to accounting periods in terms of expenses and revenues. The accounting based effective tax rate (*AETR*) is defined as the ratio of taxes to the pre-tax accounting profit (IAS 12.86):

(6.9) $$AETR = \frac{Taxes}{Pre - tax\ accounting\ profit}$$

Formally, the accounting based *AETR* is similar to the cash flow based *ETR*. Both tax rates relate taxes to a pre-tax profit. As opposed to the *ETR*, the *AETR* is not based on future cash flows and on economic profit but on the figures of a financial statement and on accounting profit.

Temporary Differences

The numerator of the *AETR* displays current taxes and deferred taxes, because IAS 12 defines tax expense (tax income) as the aggregate amount of current and deferred taxes. Current taxes encompass the taxes paid (refunded) and the tax liabilities accrued in the accounting period. Deferred taxes are the amounts of income taxes payable or recoverable in future periods in respect of taxable temporary differences.

Deferred taxes have their origin in temporary differences between the tax computation and financial accounting. Deferred taxes come into play if a company's revenues and expenses enter both the tax base and the financial accounts, but in different periods. Temporary differences reverse over time. Temporary differences may be generated, for example, by different depreciation rules in tax law (e.g. straight line) and financial accounting (e.g. declining balance). As a result, the taxable profit of a year deviates from the accounting profit and current taxes may improperly relate to accounting profit, showing a tax burden which is either too low or too high.

By taking into account deferred taxes, a misrepresentation of the company's tax burden is avoided. In effect, financial accounting synchronizes the tax expenses and the pre-tax profit to produce a meaningful tax burden. Capital market investors using accounting information in the valuation process of the company's shares are provided with an after-tax accounting profit which is not distorted by temporary differences between tax accounting and financial accounting.

Temporary Differences versus Permanent Differences

Deferred taxes are accounted for if the total amount of revenues and expenses related to an asset or liability in the tax computation and financial accounts is the same over time. No tax is deferred as a result of differences between accounting profit and taxable income that will not reverse in a later period, i.e. where the total amount of revenues and expenses is not the same over time.

Indeed, there are many such permanent differences between taxable income and the financial profit. Permanent differences have their origin in revenues which are not taxable (e.g. tax-free dividends) or in expenses which are not tax-deductible (e.g. fines).

Expenses which will never be tax-deductible increase the accounting based effective tax rate. Revenues which are tax-free per se decrease the accounting based effective tax rate.

6.3. Determination of Deferred Taxes

IAS 12 contains detailed rules to take account of current and future tax consequences of actual transactions. If the underlying transaction is recognized in the income statement (affecting net income), the respective tax effect is also recognized in the same income statement as well. If the underlying transaction is recognized directly in equity (not affecting net income, e.g. a revaluation under IAS 16), the respective tax effect is also recognized directly in equity.

Current taxes

Current taxes are the amount of tax payable (recoverable) with respect to taxable profits (losses). Current taxes actually paid (recovered) are expenses (income). To the extent that current taxes have not yet been paid, a tax liability is taken up. A tax asset is recognized if the amount of taxes paid exceeds the amount due.

If a loss carry-back is available, the tax effect of a loss of the current period is taken up immediately as an asset if the company intends to use the loss carry-back to recover taxes of previous periods. Regarding current taxes, IAS 12 prescribes accounting procedures which are found under the local accounting principles of many countries.

Deferred Taxes

Technically, the temporary concept of IAS 12 focuses on differences of book values in the balance sheet. A temporary difference is defined as the difference between the carrying amount (book value) of an asset or liability in the financial accounts and in the tax computations (tax base). The term "tax base", which IAS 12.5 defines, denotes the tax book value of an asset or liability and should not be confused with the taxable base on which income taxes are levied. Temporary differences will be reversed and result in a deductible (taxable) amount in subsequent periods generating tax savings (tax expenses).

A deferred tax asset is recognized in the balance sheet if assets in the tax accounts have a higher book value than in the financial accounts. When the book value in the financial accounts (carrying amount) of the asset will be recovered and economic benefits will flow to the company, the difference in tax book value (tax base) and carrying amount of the asset will result in future tax savings. Correspondingly, a deferred tax asset is recognized in the balance sheet if the book value (tax base) of liabilities in the tax computations is lower than in the financial accounts (carrying amount). If the liability is to be settled through an outflow of economic resources, the difference in tax book value (tax base) of the liability and its accounting book value (carrying amount) will result in future tax savings. Taking up a deferred tax asset in the balance sheet, necessarily requires taking up the amount to deferred tax income in the income statement.

A deferred tax liability is taken up in the balance sheet if assets in the tax computations have a lower book value than in the financial accounts. When the book value in the financial accounts (carrying amount) of the asset is recovered and economic benefits flow to the company, the difference in tax book value (tax base) and carrying amount of the asset will result in future tax expenses. Correspondingly, a deferred tax liability is recognized in the balance sheet if the book value (tax base) of liabilities in the tax accounts is higher than in the financial accounts (carrying amount). When the carrying amount of the liability is settled through an outflow of economic resources, the difference in tax book value (tax base) and carrying amount of the liability will result in future tax expense. A deferred tax liability in the balance sheet necessarily implies a deferred tax expense in the income statement.

As opposed to a deferred tax liability, a deferred tax asset can only be recognized if it is probable ("more likely than not") that sufficient taxable profits will be available to absorb the reversal of the deductible temporary difference. Tax planning aimed at creating taxable profits in order to realize deferred tax assets, e. g. a sale and lease back transaction is a factor in the assessment of whether sufficient taxable profits will be available. All non-tax costs and all tax costs of the tax planning strategy have to be deducted in assessing the future taxable profits. By contrast to deferred tax assets, tax planning is not relevant to deferred tax liabilities.

Tax Losses

Deferred tax assets include the tax savings from a loss carry-forward because a loss carry-forward is an entitlement to future tax relief. But here again, it must be probable that future taxable profits will be available. Unused tax losses are considered to be strong evidence that future taxable profits will not be available to the company. Therefore, a company with a history of recent losses may recognize an asset only to the extent that there is convincing evidence that the losses can be used in the future. Evidence can be based, for instance, on a tax planning scheme designed to use the losses.

Measurement

As regards the measurement of current tax assets and tax liabilities, IAS 12 prescribes that current taxes are measured by reference to tax rates and tax laws which have been enacted or substantively enacted by the end of the reporting period. A tax law is substantively enacted if it is almost certain to be enacted, such as when the bill has already been passed by parliament and only the signature by the head of the state remains outstanding.

With respect to deferred taxes, IAS 12 prescribes that deferred taxes are measured by reference to tax rates and tax laws which are expected to apply when deferred tax assets or deferred tax liabilities are realized or settled. A company should measure deferred tax assets (tax liabilities) at those tax rates (and tax laws) that have been enacted or substantively enacted by the end of the reporting period.

Example (6.3): As in the Example (6.2), the company invests 1,000 at $t = 0$ (the beginning of year 1). Without taking into account the cost of the investment, the corporation's pre-tax profits are 600 at $t = 1$ (the end of year 1), 300 at $t = 2$ (the end of year 2), and 275 at $t = 3$ (the end of year 3). In the financial accounts, the asset is recognized in the balance sheet and depreciated on a straight-line basis; the expected useful life is 3 years. In the tax computations, the asset is immediately expensed in year 1. The company is subject to a corporation tax rate of 40%. As a result, the company receives a tax refund of 160 [= 40% · (600 - 1000)] in year 1 and pays corporation tax in the years 2 and 3 of the amount 120 (= 40% · 350) and 110 (= 40% · 275) respectively. The table displays the average effective tax rate.

t			1	2	3
1	Carrying amount end of year		666.67	333.33	0.00
2	Depreciation		333.33	333.33	333.33
3	Tax base end of year		0.00	0.00	0.00
4	Temporary difference	(1) - (3)	666.67	333.33	0.00
5	Deferred tax liability	(4) · 40%	266.67	133.33	0.00
6	Deferred tax expenses	$(5)_{t=1}$	266.67	0.00	0.00
7	Deferred tax income	$(5)_t - (5)_{t+1}$	0.00	133.33	133.33
8	Current tax expenses		0.00	120.00	110.00
9	Current tax income		160.00	0.00	0.00
10	Total tax expenses	(6) + (8)	266.67	120.00	110.00
11	Total tax income	(7) + (9)	160.00	133.33	133.33
12	Total taxes	(10) – (11)	106.67	-13.33	-23.33
13	Profit before taxes and depreciation		600.00	300.00	275.00
14	Profit before taxes after depreciation	(13) – (2)	266.67	-33.33	-58.33
15	*AETR* (%)	(12)/(14)	40.00	40.00	40.00
16	Applicable tax rate (%)		40.00	40.00	40.00

Because the carrying amount of the asset in the financial accounts (book value) exceeds the tax book value of the asset (tax base) in year 1, a deferred tax liability and deferred tax expenses are recognized in year 1. The deferred tax liability reduces to zero over time. Accordingly, deferred tax income accrues in the years 2 and 3. In the years 2 and 3, the company suffers losses because depreciation exceeds gross profits. In these years, the total tax income exceeds the total tax expenses resulting in a net tax income. The *AETR* remains constant over time at the rate of 40%, which is equal to the applicable (statutory) tax rate.

In Example (6.3), the *AETR* equals the statutory tax rate in each year, because a deferred tax liability is recognized. From an accounting perspective, the recognition of a deferred tax liability provides the shareholders with the information that the average tax burden of the company is 40%, irrespective of the temporary divergences between tax accounting and financial accounting.

Timing Effects

With a constant statutory tax rate over time, the NPV of corporation tax payments solely depends on the timing of the tax payments, giving raise to interest advantages if tax payments can be postponed or disadvantages if the payments are advanced. In Example (6.2), the timing effect reduces the company's tax burden and leads to a cash flow based effective tax rate (*ETR*) below the statutory tax rate. By contrast to the *ETR*, the accounting based *AETR* does not reveal the timing effect. In Example (6.3) the *AETR* equals the statutory tax rate, even though the company is able to significantly reduce its effective tax burden in present value terms.

IAS 12 forbids discounting of deferred taxes, stating that discounting is impracticable or at least highly complex. An option to discount deferred taxes is not available. Indeed, an option would harm the comparability of financial statements. Because deferred taxes are measured at their nominal value (product of statutory tax rate times the temporary difference), interest advantages or interest disadvantages do not influence the tax position of the company in terms of the *AETR*. Hence, IAS 12 income tax reporting fails to provide full disclosure of the company's effective tax burden. A tax planning strategy which aims at timing effects, e.g. by the utilization of favorable tax depreciation rules or by the timely utilization of a loss carry-forward, is not fully reflected in the *AETR*.

6.4. Tax Reconciliation Statement

IAS 12 provides for extensive disclosure requirements. Major components of tax expenses and tax income are to be reported separately. Important items, among others, are current tax expense or current tax income and the amount of deferred tax expense or deferred tax income relating to the arisal or reversal of temporary differences. Tax reconciliation should enable investors to understand whether the relationship between tax expense (tax income) and financial accounting profit is unusual as well as to identify important factors which affect this relationship.

An explanation of the relationship between tax expense (tax income) and the financial accounting profit is to be provided either by numerical reconciliation, by tax rate reconciliation or by both types of reconciliation. Numerical reconciliation refers to the tax expense (tax income) and the product of accounting profit multiplied by the applicable tax rate. Tax rate reconciliation refers to the average effective tax rate and the applicable tax rate.

The starting point of tax reconciliation is the applicable tax rate, which is determined either by the tax rate of the country where a subsidiary resides (separate reconciliations for each entity), or by the domestic tax rate of the country where the parent company has its tax residence (home-based approach). The applicable tax rate is then compared to the group's effective tax rate (*AETR*). This comparison shows whether the company has successfully reduced its tax burden (applicable tax rate is higher than the *AETR*) or has suffered from a further charge over the applicable tax rate (applicable tax rate is lower than the *AETR*).

The tax reconciliation shows, in particular, international tax rate differentials, permanent differences between the taxable base and the accounting profit, tax losses, and deferred taxes.

Example (6.4): G Corporation is a multinational company, resident in country G. G Corporation discloses in year 1 an income before taxes of € 4,000 and tax expenses of € 800 € resulting in a net income of € 3,200. G Corporation uses the home based approach for tax rate reconciliation. G Corporation's statutory corporate income tax rate amounts to 30%. The table displays the reconciliation from the statutory tax rate in country G to the effective tax rate.

	Year 1	
	€	%
Profit before tax	4,000	-
Expected corporation tax in country G	1,200	30.00
Foreign tax rate differential	-300	-7.50
Tax exempt income	-200	-5.00
Non-deductible expenses	50	1.25
Deferred tax liabilities	50	1.25
Income taxes (*AETR*)	800	20.00

In country G, a uniform corporation tax rate of 30% is levied, resulting in an expected corporation tax of € 1,200 (= 4,000 · 30%). The taxes of foreign group companies are assessed at the rates applicable locally, which results in a foreign tax rate differential reducing the effective tax rate. Tax exempt income, e.g. inter-corporate dividends, reduces the effective tax rate. Non-deductible expenses increase the effective tax rate. Higher carrying amounts of the assets than the assets' tax bases may entail deferred tax liabilities which increase the effective tax rate. G Corporation's effective tax rate (*AETR*) of 20.00% falls short of the applicable tax rate of 30%, indicating that G Corporation has successfully managed to reduce the group's tax burden on the accounting profit of € 4,000.

Important factors increasing the *AETR* are tax loss carry-forwards which cannot be deducted from future profits and non-deductible expenses. Important factors reducing the *AETR* are tax-free income and tax loss carry-forwards which can be used in the future.

6.5. Effective Tax Rate and International Tax Planning

Financial statements under IFRS are mostly prepared by multinational companies. These companies are able to engage in international tax planning by either shifting profits or shifting real investments to low-tax countries. The decision to locate profitable real investments in low-tax countries is mainly driven by the statutory tax rate. Profit shifting is exclusively driven by differences in statutory tax rates. Tax accounting rules and timing effects are of minor importance.

If a company's tax planning strategy aims at exploiting international differences in statutory tax rates, IAS 12 income tax reporting, which ignores timing effects, can be expected to provide meaningful information to both the company's management and the shareholders.

Permanent Differences

The applicable (statutory) profit tax rate in the residence country of the parent company indicates the potential amount of tax savings through profit and investment shifting to foreign low-tax countries. International tax planning should in particular focus on permanent differences reducing the *AETR*.

Permanent differences arise if foreign profits earned by permanent establishments are exempted from the income tax base of the principal company in the home country. Foreign subsidiaries' profits are also not included in the income tax base of the domestic parent company. Distributed profits of foreign subsidiaries are excluded from the parent company's tax base if the parent company's country of residence applies the exemption method for the dividends received. As a result, low foreign taxes can be exploited by parent companies resident in exemption countries (e.g. Germany, France, and the Netherlands), whereas parent companies resident in credit countries (e.g. the U.S.) may face additional taxes upon repatriation of profits.

Tax Planning and the AETR

The *AETR* can be reduced, for example, by equity financing the investments of foreign subsidiaries located in countries with low tax rates, by transfer of business functions to low-taxed foreign subsidiaries, by book profit shifting to low-taxed foreign subsidiaries through transfer pricing and debt financing. By interposing a financing company located in a low-tax country, a parent company can obtain access to low foreign taxes even if the investments are located in high-tax countries. In such a case, the legal structure of a multinational group serves the purpose of reducing the company's *AETR*.

In summary, the company's tax management should primarily focus on tax planning strategies which impact on the *AETR* under IAS 12. Because temporary differences do not affect the *AETR* under IAS 12, tax planning strategies of a multinational company need not take timing effects into account. On the other hand, timing effects definitely affect the companies' net cash flow. Therefore, it seems unlikely that companies reporting under IFRS will completely ignore tax deferral effects.

Reading List Chapter 6

Devereux, Michael P; Griffith, Rachel: Evaluating Tax Policy for Location Decisions, in: International Tax and Public Finance 2003, pp.107-126.

Dixon, John; Finney, Malcolm (eds.): International Corporate Tax Planning, London, 2002.

Epstein, Barry J.; Jermakovizc, Eva K.: Wiley Interpretation and Application of International Financial Reporting Standards 2010, 7th Edition, Hoboken, 2010.

Jacobs, Otto H.; Spengel, Christoph: Measurements and Development of the Effective Tax Burden of Companies – An Overview and International Comparison, in: Intertax 2000, pp. 334-351.

Kieso, Donald E.; Weygandt, Jerry J.; Warfield, Terry D.: Intermediate Accounting, 14th Edition, Hoboken, 2012.

King, Mervyn A.; Fullerton, Don: The Taxation of Income from Capital, Chicago, 1984.

Müller, Jens; Sureth, Caren: The Impact of Tax optimized Investment Projects on the Effective Group Tax Rate, in: Die Betriebswirtschaft 2010, pp. 331-348.

PricewaterhouseCoopers: Global Effective Tax Rates, 2011.

Ruf, Martin: The Economic Unit of Effective Tax Rates; in: World Tax Journal 2011, pp. 226-246.

Samuelson, Paul A.: Tax Deductibility of Economic Depreciation to Insure Invariant Valuations, in: The Journal of Political Economy 1964, pp. 604-606.

Schreiber, Ulrich; Spengel, Christoph; Lammersen, Lothar: Measuring the Impact of Taxation on Investment and Financing Decisions, in: Schmalenbach Business Review 2002, pp. 2-23.

Scholes, Myron S.; Wolfson, Mark A.; Erickson, Merle; Maydew, Edward L.; Shevlin; Terry: Taxes and Business Strategy, 4th Edition; Upper Saddle River New Jersey, 2009.

Sørensen, Peter B.: Company Tax Reform in the European Union, in: International Tax and Public Finance 2004, pp. 91-115.

Spengel, Christoph: International Accounting Standards, Tax Accounting and Effective Levels of Company Tax Burden in the EU, in: European Taxation 2003, pp.253-266.

Literature

Agúendez-Garcia, Ana: The Delineation and Apportionment of an EU Consolidated Tax Base for Multi-Jurisdictual Corporate Income Taxation, European Commission Working Paper No. 9, 2006.

Amatucci, Andrea: International Tax Law, Alphen aan den Rijn, 2006.

Ault, Huge J.; Arnold, Brian, J.: Comparative Income Taxation. A Structural Analysis, 3rd ed. Alphen aan den Rijn, 2010.

Avery Jones, John F.: Avoiding Double Taxation: Credit versus Exemption - the Origins, in: Bulletin for International Taxation 2012, pp. 67-76.

Avi-Yonah, Reuven S.; Benshalom, Ilan: Formulary Apportionment – Myths and Prospects. Promoting Better International Tax Policies by Utilizing the Misunderstood and Under-Theorized Formulary Alternative, in: World Tax Journal 2011, pp. 371-398.

Bittker, Boris I.; Eustice, James S.; Goldstein, Gersham: Federal Income Taxation of Corporation and Shareholders, 7th Edition, Warren Gorham & Lamont, New York, 2000.

Brealey, Richard A.; Myers, Stewart C.: Principles of Corporate Finance, 9th Edition, New York, 2007.

Brosens, Linda: Thin Capitalization Rules and EU Law, in: EC Tax Review 2004, pp. 188-213.

Büttner, Thies; Overesch, Michael; Schreiber, Ulrich; Wamser, Georg: The Impact of Thin- Capitalization Rules on the Capital Structure of Multinational Firms, in: Journal of Public Economics, published online 13.07.12.

Büttner, Thies; Overesch, Michael; Schreiber, Ulrich; Wamser, Georg: Taxation and Capital Structure Choice - Evidence from a Panel of German Multinationals, in: Economics Letters 105(3), 2009, pp. 309-311.

Clausing, Kimberly A.: International tax avoidance and U.S. international trade, National Tax Journal 2006, pp. 269-287.

Clausing, Kimberly A.: Tax-Motivated Transfer Pricing and US Intrafirm Trade Prices, in: Journal of Public Economics 2003, pp. 2207-2223.

Clausing, Kimberly A.: The impact of transfer pricing on intrafirm trade, in: J.R. Hines (ed.), International taxation and multinational activity, Chicago, 2001, pp. 173-194.

Cnossen, Sijbren (ed.): Taxing Capital Income in the European Union: Issues and Options for Reform, Oxford, 2000.

Cordewener; Axel; Pistone, Pasquale; Reimer, Ekkehart; Romano, Carlo: The Tax Treatment of Foreign Losses: Ritter, M&S, and the Way ahead, in: European Taxation 2004; pp. 135-142; pp. 218-233.

Desai, Mihir A.; Hines, James R.: Evaluating International Tax Reform, in: National Tax Journal 2003, pp. 487-502.

Desai, Mihir A.; Foley, Fritz; Hines, James R.: A Multinational Perspective on Capital Structure Choice and Internal Capital Markets, in: The Journal of Finance 2004, pp. 2451-2487.

Devereux, Michael P.: Business taxation in a globalized world, in: Oxford Review of Economic Policy 2008, pp. 625–638.

Devereux, Michael P.: Debating Proposed Reforms of the Taxation of Corporate Income in the European Union, in: International Tax and Public Finance, 2004, pp. 71-89.

Devereux, Michael P.; Griffith, Rachel: Evaluating Tax Policy for Location Decisions, in: International Tax and Public Finance 2003, pp. 107-126.

Devereux, Michael P.; Griffith, Rachel: Taxes and the location of production: Evidence from a panel of US multinationals, Journal of Public Economics 1998, pp. 335-367.

Devereux Michael P., Sørensen Peter B.: The corporate income tax: international trends and options for fundamental reform. Economic papers, Brussels 2006.

Dixon, John; Finney, Malcolm (eds.): International Corporate Tax Planning, London, 2002.

Elschner, Christina; Spengel, Christoph: R&D Tax Incentives: Empirical Evidence, International Comparison and Reform Options for Germany, in: Zeitschrift für Betriebswirtschaft 2010, Special Issue 2, pp. 1-22.

Endres, Dieter; Oestreicher, Andreas, Scheffler; Wolfram; Spengel, Christoph et al.: The Determination of Corporate Taxable Income in the EU Member States, Kluwer Law International, Alphen aan den Rijn, 2007.

Endres, Dieter; Spengel, Christoph; Brunsbach, Stefan; Miles, Andrew: Unternehmensbesteuerung in Deutschland, Corporate Taxation in Germany, 3rd Edition, Düsseldorf, 2012.

Epstein, Barry J.; Jermakovizc, Eva K.: Wiley Interpretation and Application of International Financial Reporting Standards 2010, 7th Edition, Hoboken, 2010.

Ernst & Young: Precision under Pressure - Global Transfer Pricing Survey 2007-2008, 2007.

Ernst & Young: 2009 Global Transfer Pricing Survey - Tax Authority Insights, Perspectives, Interpretations and Regulatory Changes, 2009.

European Commission: Proposal for a Council Directive on a Common Consolidated Corporate Tax Base (CCCTB), COM (2011) 212/4, Brussels, 2011.

European Commission: European Tax Survey, Working Paper 3/2004, Office for Official Publications of the European Communities, Luxembourg, 2004.

European Commission: Company Taxation in the Internal Market, Commission Staff Working paper, Luxembourg, 2002.

Federal Ministry of Finance, Bundesministerium der Finanzen, Die wichtigsten Steuern im internationalen Vergleich, Berlin, 2012.

Finnerty, Chris; Merks, Paulus; Petriccione, Mario; Russo, Raffeale: Fundamentals of International Tax Planning, Amsterdam, 2007.

Frenkel, Jacob A.; Razin, Assaf; Sadka, Efraim: International Taxation in an Integrated World, Cambridge, 1991.

Führich, Gregor: Exit Taxation and ECJ case law, in: European Taxation 2008, pp. 10-19.

Fuest, Clemens; Hemmelgarn, Thomas; Ramb, Fred: "How Would the Introduction of an EU-wide Formula Apportionment Affect the Distribution and Size of the Corporate Tax Base? An Analysis Based on German Multinationals", in: International Tax and Public Finance 2007, pp. 627-648.

Gammie, Malcolm: The Role of the European Court of Justice in the Development of Direct Taxation in the European Union, in: Bulletin for International Fiscal Documentation 2003, pp. 86-98.

Gammie, Malcolm; Giannini, Silvia; Klemm, Alexander; Oestreicher, Andreas; Parancandolo, Paola; Spengel, Christoph: Achieving a Common Consolidated Corporate Tax Base in the EU, 2006.

Grubert, Harry: Intangible Income, Intercompany Transactions, Income Shifting, and the Choice of Location, in: National Tax Journal 2003, pp. 221-242.

Haig, Robert M.: The Concept of Income: Economic and Legal Aspects, in: Haig, Robert M.: The Federal Income Tax, New York, 1921.

Hebous, Shafik; Ruf, Martin; Weichenrieder, Alfons: The Effects of Taxation on the Location Decisions of Multinational Firms: M&A vs. Greenfield Investments; CESifo Working Paper. 3076, 2010.

Hellerstein, Jerome R.; Hellerstein, Walter: State Taxation, 3rd Edition, Boston, 2007.

Hellerstein, Walter; McLure, Charles E. Jr.: The European Commission's Report on Company Income Taxation: What the EU can Learn from the Experience of the US States, in: International Tax and Public Finance 2004, pp. 199-220.

Hines, James: Lessons from the Behavioral Responses to International Taxation, in: National Tax Journal 1997, pp. 305 – 322.

Hirshleifer, Jack: On the Economics of Transfer Pricing, in: The Journal of Business 1956, pp. 172-184.

Homburg, Stefan: Competition and Co-ordination in International Capital Income Taxation, FinanzArchiv 1999, pp. 1 – 17.

Huinzinga, Harry; Laeven, Luc.; Nicodéme, Gaetan: Capital Structure and International Debt Shifting in Europe, Journal of Financial Economics 2008, pp. 80-118.

Huizinga, Harry; Voget, Johannes: International taxation and the direction and volume of cross-border M&As, Journal of Finance 2009, pp. 1217-1249.

Helminen, Marjaana: Is there a Future for CFC-Regimes in the EU?, in: International Tax review 2005, pp. 117-123.

IBFD: Taxation of Companies in Europe, Amsterdam, 2009.

Jacobs, Otto H.; Endres, Dieter; Spengel, Christoph (eds.): Internationale Unternehmensbesteuerung, 7th Edition, München, 2011.

Jacobs, Otto H.; Spengel, Christoph: Measurements and Development of the EffectiveTax Burden of Companies – An Overview and International Comparison; in: Intertax 2000, pp. 334-351.

Jog, Vijay; Tang, Jianmin: Tax Reforms, Debt Shifting and Tax Revenue: Multinational Corporations in Canada, International Tax and Public Finance 2001, pp. 5-25.

Kieso, Donald E.; Weygandt, Jerry J.; Warfield, Terry D.: Intermediate Accounting, 14th Edition, Hoboken, 2012.

King, Mervyn A.; Fullerton, Don: The Taxation of Income from Capital; Chicago, 1984.

Koch, Reinald; Spengel, Christoph; Oestreicher, Andreas: How to Reform Taxation of Corporate Groups in Europe, in: World Tax Journal 2011, pp. 5-38.

Kofler, Georg: Indirect Credit versus Exemption: Double Taxation Relief for Intercompany Distributions, in: Bulletin for International Taxation 2012, pp. 77-89.

Kruschwitz, Lutz; Löffler, Andreas: Discounted Cash Flow – A Theory of the Valuation of Firms; Chichester, 2006.

Lang, Michael: Introduction to the Law of Double Taxation Conventions, Vienna, 2010.

Lang, Michael; Aigner, Hans-Jörgen; Scheuerle, Ulrich; Stefaner, Markus: CFC Legislation – Domestic Provisions, Tax Treaties and EC Law, Vienna, 2004.

Lang, Michael; Pistone, Pasquale; Schuch, Josef; Staringer, Claus: Introduction to European Tax Law on Direct Taxation, 2nd Edition, Vienna, 2010.

Lang, Michael; Pistone, Pasquale; Schuch, Josef; Staringer, Claus: Common Consolidated Corporate Tax Base, Vienna, 2008.

Lodin, Sven-Olof; Gammie, Malcolm: Home State Taxation, Amsterdam, 2001.

Luckhaupt, Hagen; Overesch, Michael; Schreiber, Ulrich: The OECD Approach to Transfer Pricing. A Critical Assessment and Proposal, in: Schön, Wolfgang; Konrad, Kai A. (eds.), MPI Studies in Tax Law and Public Finance 1, Fundamentals of International Transfer Pricing in Law and Economics, München, 2012, S. 91-121.

Lüdicke, Jürgen: Exemption and Tax Credit in German Tax Treaties – Policy and Reality, in Bulletin for International Taxation 2010, pp. 609-619.

Martens-Weiner, Joann: Company Tax Reform in the European Union. Guidance from the United States and Canada on Implementing Formulary Apportionment in the EU, New York, 2006.

McLure, Charles E. Jr.: Corporate Tax Harmonization in the European Union: The Commission's Proposals, in: Tax Notes International 2004, pp. 775–801.

Meussen, Gerard: Cross-Border Loss Compensation, and Permanent Establishments: Lidl Belgium and Deutsche Shell, in: European Taxation 2008, pp. 233-236.

Meussen, Gerard: The Principle of Equality in European Taxation, London, 1999.

Miller, Angharad; Oats, Lynne: Principles of International Taxation, West Sussex, 2009.

Mintz, Jack: Corporate Tax Harmonization in Europe: It's All About Compliance, in: International Tax and Public Finance 2004, pp. 221-234.

Müller, Jens; Sureth, Caren: The Impact of Tax Optimized Investment Projects on the Effective Group Tax Rate, in: Die Betriebswirtschaft 2010, pp. 331-348.

Munin, Nellie: Tax in Troubled Time: Is it the Time for a Common Consolidated Corporate Tax Base in the EU, in: EC Tax Review 2011, pp. 121-133.

Musgrave, Peggy B. (ed.): Tax Policy in the Global Economy, Cheltenham/Northhampton, 2002.

Mogdialiani, Franco; Miller, Merton H.: The Cost of Capital, Corporation Finance, and the Theory of Investment, American Economic Review 1958, pp. 261-297.

Nocke Volker; Yeaple, Stephen: An Assignment Theory of Foreign Direct Investment, Review of Economic Studies 2008, pp. 529-557.

OECD: Transfer Pricing Guidelines for Multinational Enterprises and Tax Administrations 2010, Paris, 2010.

OECD: Model Tax Convention on Income and Capital, Paris, 2010.

OECD: International Tax Avoidance and Evasion – Four Related Studies, Paris, 1987.

Oestreicher, Andreas; Reister, Timo; Spengel, Christoph: Common Corporate Tax Base and Effective Tax Burdens in the EU Member States, in: World Tax Journal 2009, pp. 44-66.

Oestreicher, Andreas; Spengel, Christoph: Tax Harmonization in Europe: The Determination of Corporate Taxable Income in the Member States, in: European Taxation 2007, pp. 437-451.

Overesch, Michael: The Effects of Multinationals′ Profit Shifting Activities on Real Investments, National Tax Journal, 2009, pp. 5-23.

Overesch, Michael; Schreiber, Ulrich: Asset Specifity, International Profit Shifting, and Investment Decisions, Zeitschrift für Betriebswirtschaft 2010, Special Issue 2, pp. 23-47.

Overesch, Michael; Wamser, Georg; Who cares about Corporate Taxation? Asymmetric Tax Effects on Outbound FDI, in: World Economy 2009, pp. 1657-1684.

Peeters, Bruno: The Concept of Tax, EATLP Congress 2005, Naples, 2005.

PricewaterhouseCoopers: Global Effective Tax Rates, 2011.

Raff, Horst; Ryan, Michael; Stähler, Frank: The choice of market entry mode: Greenfield investment, M&A and joint venture, in: International Review of Economics and Finance 2009, pp. 3-10.

Ruf, Martin: The Economic Unit of Effective Tax Rates; in: World Tax Journal 2011, pp. 226-246.

Ruf, Martin: Why is the Response of Multinationals Capital Structure Choice to Tax Incentives That Low? Some Possible Explanations; in: Finanzarchiv 2011, pp. 123-144.

Russo, Raffaele (ed.): Fundamentals of International Tax Planning, Amsterdam, 2007.

Samuelson, Paul A.: Tax Deductibility of Economic Depreciation to Insure Invariant Valuations, in: The Journal of Political Economy 1964, pp. 604-606.

Schanz, Deborah; Schanz, Sebastian: Business Taxation and Financial Decisions, Heidelberg, 2011.

Schmalenbach, Eugen: Pretiale Wirtschaftslenkung, Volume 1, Die optimale Geltungszahl Bremen et al., 1947.

Schön, Wolfgang; Schreiber, Ulrich; Spengel, Christoph: A Common Consolidated Corporate Tax Base for Europe, Heidelberg, 2008.

Scholes, Myron S.; Wolfson, Mark A.; Erickson, Merle; Maydew, Edward L.; Shevlin, Terry: Taxes and Business Strategy, 4th Edition, Upper Saddle River, New Jersey, 2009.

Schreiber, Ulrich: The Taxation of Hidden Reserves under the Common Consolidated Corporate Tax Base, in: European Taxation 2009, pp. 84-91.

Schreiber, Ulrich; Führich, Gregor: European group taxation - the role of exit taxes, in: European Journal of Law and Economics 2009, pp. 257-274.

Schreiber, Ulrich; Spengel, Christoph; Lammersen, Lothar: Measuring the Impact of Taxation on Investment and Financing Decisions, in: Schmalenbach Business Review 2002, pp. 2-23.

Shackelford, Douglas A., Shevlin, Terry: Empirical tax research in accounting, in: Journal of Accounting and Economics 2001, pp. 321–387.

Sinn, Hans W.: Capital Income Taxation and Resource Allocation, North Holland, Amsterdam, New York, Oxford and Tokio, 1987.

Slemrod, Joel B.: Free Trade Taxation and Protectionist Taxation, in: International Tax and Public Finance 1995, pp. 471-489.

Sørensen, Peter B.: Company Tax Reform in the European Union, in: International Tax and Public Finance 2004, pp. 91-115.

Spengel, Christoph: International Accounting Standards, Tax Accounting and Effective Levels of Company Tax Burden in the EU, in: European Taxation 2003, pp. 253-266.

Spengel, Christoph; Oestreicher, Andreas; Koch, Reinald: How to Reform Taxation of Corporate Groups in Europe, in: World Tax Journal 2011, pp. 5-38.

Spengel, Christoph; Zöllkau, York: Common Corporate Tax Base (CC(C)TB) and Determination of Taxable Income. An International Comparison, Heidelberg, 2012.

Tanzi, Vito: Taxation in an Integrated World, Washington, 1995.

Terra, Ben J.M.; Wattel, Peter J.: European Tax Law 5th Edition, Alphen aan den Rijn 2008.

van Boeijen-Ostaszewska, Ola; Schellekens, Marnix (eds.): European Tax Handbook 2012, Amsterdam, 2012.

Vermeend, Willem; Van der Ploeg, Rick; Timmer; Jan Willem: Taxes and the Economy 2008, Cheltenham.

Vogel, Klaus: Klaus Vogel on Double Taxation Conventions, 3rd Edition, London, 1997.

Vogel, Klaus: Worldwide vs. Source Taxation of Income – A review and re-evaluation of arguments (Part I, II, III), Intertax 1988, pp. 216-229; pp. 310-320; pp. 393-402.

Zodrow, George R.: On the "Traditional" and "New" Views of Dividend Taxation, in: National Tax Journal 1991, pp. 497-509.

European Court of Justice:

Dassonville	8/74	ECR 1974	pp. 837 -866
Daily Mail	81/87	ECR 1988	pp. 5483-5514
Bachmann	C-204/90	ECR I-1992	pp. 249-286
Schumacker	C-279/93	ECR I-1995	pp. 225-268
Gebhard	C-55/94	ECR I-1995	pp. 4165-4201
Asscher	C-107/94	ECR I-1996	pp. 3089-3132
Leur-Blom	C-28/95	ECR I-1997	pp. 4161-4208
Futura	C-250/95	ECR I-1997	pp. 2471-2506
Saint-Gobain	C-307/97	ECR I-1999	pp. 6161-6206
Verkooijen	C-35/98	ECR I-2000	pp. 4071-4137
Metallgesellschaft	C-397/98	ECR I-2001	pp. 1727-1794
Metallgesellschaft	C-410/98	ECR I-2001	pp. 1727-1794
Amid	C-141/99	ECR I-2000	pp. 11619-11645
Lankhorst-Hohorst	C-324/00	ECR I-2002	pp. 11779-11817

Bosal	C-168/01	ECR I-2003	pp. 9409-9447
De Lasteyrie du Saillant	C-9/02	ECR I-2004	pp. 2409-2460
Manninen	C-319/02	ECR I-2004	pp. 7477-7515
Marks & Spencer	C-446/03	ECR I-2005	pp. 10837-10886
Cadburry Schweppes	C-194/04	ECR I-2006	pp. 7995-8054
Meilicke	C-292/04	ECR I-2007	pp. 1835-1890
Oy AA	C-231/05	ECR I-2007	pp. 6373-6414
Lidl Belgium	C-414/06	ECR I-2008	pp. 3601-3634

German Federal Fiscal Court:

BFH	I R 100/09	BStB II 2010	p. 1065

Index

A

Acquisition 5, 35, 38, 51, 58, 59, 60, 61, 63, 78, 79, 93, 94, 109, 110, 112, 120, 127, 137
- Maximum price buyer 38, 59, 60, 61, 62
- Minimum price seller 1, 38, 59, 60, 61, 62
- Tax planning 63
- Tax wedge 61, 62

Affiliation privilege 8, 15
Anti-abuse rules 46
- Controlled foreign corporations 48, 88, 132
- Interest stripping rule 49, 82, 83, 111
- Thin capitalization 48, 108

Arm‘s length principle 17
Asset deal 5, 129

B

Ban on discrimination 101
Bosal 110, 116, 157

C

Cadbury Schweppes 111
Capital export neutrality 37, 102
Capital import neutrality 40, 102
Cassis de Dijon formula 101
Choice of investment location 55
Choice of legal form 52
Common Consolidated Corporate Tax Base 37, 117, 133, 134, 152, 153, 154, 155, 156
- Asset relocation rule 127
- Business reorganizations 130
- Consolidation 121
- Formula apportionment 118
- Non-EU countries 117, 131, 132, 133
- Proposed rules 128
- Safeguard clause 127
- Scope of the group 119
- Tax accounting rules 120
- Tax base 118
- Transfer of assets 127
- Transfer of shares 129

Controlled foreign corporations 48, 88, 111, 112
- EU law 111

Corporation Tax
- Classical systems 8
- Depreciation 4
- Double taxation avoidance systems 8
- Double taxation mitigation systems 8
- Shareholder relief 2, 9, 10, 80, 107, 108
- Tax base 4
- Tax rates 6
- Tax system 8

Corporations
- Legal status 1
- Shareholder contracts 2
- Subsidiary 18
- Tax burden in Europe 7

Credit method 15, 16, 36, 47, 53, 74, 75, 132
- Excess credit 16, 43, 66, 75, 91
- Income basket-limitation 16
- Ordinary credit 16
- Per country limitation 16

Cross-border reorganization
- Cross-border mergers 23
- Transfer of seat 22

D

Dassonville formula 101
Discrimination
- Covert 101
- Overt 101
Double tax treaty 13
- OECD model treaty 14
Double taxation
- Economic 1, 2, 3, 8, 15, 107, 121, 128
- Legal 12, 13, 15, 51, 74
- Measures to Avoid Legal Double Taxation 13

E

Economic depreciation 137
Economic profit 136, 137, 138, 139, 141
Effective tax rate 1, 51, 135, 136, 138, 139, 140, 141, 144, 145, 146, 147
- Accounting based 140, 141, 144, 145, 146, 147, 148
- Cash flow based 136
Empirical tax research 94, 97, 156
Exemption method 15, 36, 43, 44, 45, 47, 73, 74, 105, 132, 147
Exit taxation 22, 23, 24, 76, 77, 79, 112, 113, 114, 128, 131
- EU law 113

F

Final withholding tax 53
Finance companies 90, 91, 111, 112
- Restrictions 91
Financial accounting 10, 94, 118, 119, 121, 135, 141, 145, 146
Financing decisions
- Debt financing 32
- Equity financed 28
- EU law 108, 110
- External debt 83
- Internal debt 48, 49, 79, 80, 81, 84, 95, 108, 109, 111, 132
- Shareholder debt financing 33
First-in first-out 120
Formula apportionment 118, 121, 125, 126, 127, 133
- European formula 122
- Macroeconomic factors 122
- Microeconomic factors 122
- Tax planning 125
Free capital movement 107
Freedom of establishment 99, 100, 101, 102, 104, 106, 108, 109, 110, 111, 113
- Scope 100
Fundamental economic freedoms 36, 99

G

Generally Accepted Accounting Principles 4
Goodwill 5, 23, 121, 128
Group Taxation
- Aggregation systems 11
- Full tax consolidation 11
- Group contribution 11
- Group relief system 11
- Requierements 10

H

Hidden reserves 22, 23, 24, 76, 77, 79, 112, 113, 114, 121, 127, 128, 129, 130, 131
Holding companies 92, 93
- Acquisition 93
- Debt 93
- Loss compensation 92
Holding company 93, 110
Hybrid tax system 42, 45, 46

I

Intellectual property 63, 64, 65, 66
Interest and Royalties Directive 36, 67, 80
Interest stripping rule 49, 110
International Financial Reporting Standards 118, 121, 135, 147, 148, 152
International tax arbitrage 49, 51, 84, 99, 110, 130
Investment
- Marginal 28, 30, 38, 40, 55, 57, 68, 84, 86
- Profitable 57, 76

J

Justifications 102
- Accepted 103
- Rejected 102

L

Lankhorst-Hohorst 108, 116, 157
Lidl Belgium 106, 115, 116, 155, 158
Limited tax liability 11, 12, 13, 17, 23, 24, 43, 45, 52, 53, 55, 73, 80, 118
Lock-in effect 77
Lock-out effect 77
Loss compensation 67
- EU law 104
- Immediate loss deduction 70
- Loss carry-forward 6, 67, 68, 69, 70, 105, 106, 143, 145

M

Manninen 107, 116, 157
Marks & Spencer 104, 106, 116, 157
Meilicke 107, 116, 158
Mergers Directive 23, 79, 130

N

National Grid Indus 113
Net present value 27
- Cash flow effect 28, 68, 70
- Interest effect 28, 39, 70
- Tax rate effect 30, 56, 57, 58, 76, 81

Net present value after taxes 28
Net principle 4, 5, 6, 120
Non-restriction approach 101

O

OECD model treaty 14, 15, 18, 20, 52, 76
Outbound transfer of assets 76
- Tax deferral 79

Ownership neutrality 38, 39, 41
Ownership rights 38, 39, 41, 42, 46, 51, 58, 63

P

Parent Subsidiary Directive 36, 53, 61
Partnership 1, 3, 4, 51, 105
- Legal status 3
- Partner Contracts 3

Pass-Through Entities 3
Permanent differences 141, 146, 147
Permanent establishment 52
- Definition 17
- EU law 105
- Transfer prices 20

Preliminary ruling proceeding 100
Profit repatriation 86
Profit shifting 18, 46, 70, 71, 82, 95, 108, 125, 131, 148
Proportionality 103, 112, 113

R

Realization principle 4, 22, 112, 118, 120
Research and development 63, 64, 65, 66, 95, 96, 152
Residence-based taxation 37, 39, 44, 45, 46

S

Safeguard clause 127
Separate entity accounting 18, 117, 119, 131
Share deal 61, 62, 93, 129, 130
Shareholder taxation
- EU law 107

Societas Europaea 23
Source-based taxation 41, 42
Subsidiary 52

T

Tax accounting 118, 135, 147
- Current taxes 142
- Deferred tax 142
- Tax losses 143
- Tax reconciliation 146

Tax fraud 47

Tax liability
- Limited 12
- Unlimited 12

Tax planning 47
- Acquisition 58
- Common Consolidated Corporate Tax Base 125, 128, 129, 130, 131
- Effective tax rate 148
- Empirical evidence 94
- EU law 105, 106, 108, 109, 110, 112, 114
- Finance companies 90
- Financing 80
- Holding companies 92
- Legal form 52
- Location 55
- Loss compensation 67
- Outbound transfer of assets 76
- Ownership rights 63
- Tasks 51
- Tax accounting 135
- Transfer prices 70

Tax shield 32, 35, 80, 81, 82, 93, 109
Temporary differences 141, 145, 148
Thin capitalization 48, 82, 84, 108
Timing effect 30, 57, 58, 61, 69, 76, 83, 145
Trade tax 6, 30, 31, 34, 53, 82, 84, 85
- Local multiplier 6

Transfer prices 17
- Comparable uncontrolled price method 19
- Cost-plus method 19
- Formula allocation 21
- Frictions 72
- Resale price method 19
- Restrictions 72
- Transactional net margin method 19
- Transactional profit split method 20

Treaty on the Functioning of the European Union 36, 99

U

Unitary Taxation 119
Unlimited tax liability 11, 12, 13, 17, 22, 23, 43, 52, 53, 56, 80, 107

W

Withholding tax 8, 9, 12, 13, 14, 36, 53, 54, 80, 107
Worldwide income principle 12, 16, 37

MIX
Papier aus verantwortungsvollen Quellen
Paper from responsible sources
FSC® C105338

Printed by Books on Demand, Germany